RIGHTS FORFEITURE AND PUNISHMENT

RIGHTS FORFEITURE AND PUNISHMENT

Christopher Heath Wellman

OXFORD
UNIVERSITY PRESS

OXFORD
UNIVERSITY PRESS

Oxford University Press is a department of the University of Oxford. It furthers the University's objective of excellence in research, scholarship, and education by publishing worldwide. Oxford is a registered trade mark of Oxford University Press in the UK and certain other countries.

Published in the United States of America by Oxford University Press
198 Madison Avenue, New York, NY 10016, United States of America.

Library of Congress Cataloging-in-Publication Data
Names: Wellman, Christopher Heath, author.
Title: Rights forfeiture and punishment / Christopher Heath Wellman.
Description: New York : Oxford University Press, 2017.
Identifiers: LCCN 2016048540 | ISBN 9780190274764 (hardcover : alk. paper)
Subjects: LCSH: Punishment. | Human rights. | Justice, Administration of.
Classification: LCC HV7419 .W445 2017 | DDC 364.6/8—dc23
LC record available at https://lccn.loc.gov/2016048540

1 3 5 7 9 8 6 4 2
Printed by Sheridan Books, Inc., United States of America

For Padre

CONTENTS

ACKNOWLEDGMENTS

I have been working on these issues for several years now, so in addition to numerous helpful discussions with academic audiences, I am deeply indebted to many friends and colleagues for their generous feedback. In particular, I would like to thank Nate Adams, Larry Alexander, Andrew Altman, Scott Baker, Christian Barry, Mitch Berman, Jacob Bronsther, Eric Brown, Kimberley Brownlee, William Bulow, Vincent Chaio, Andrew Cornford, Alan Cromartie, Richard Dagger, John Deigh, Julia Driver, Antony Duff, James Edwards, Lindsay Farmer, Kim Ferzan, John Gardner, David Gilboa, Stuart Green, Brad Hooker, Zachary Hoskins, Douglas Husak, Stephen Kershnar, Christopher Kutz, Seth Lazar, Ambrose Lee, David Lefkowitz, Loren Lomasky, Eric Mack, Catriona McKinnon, Sandra Marshall, Jeff McMahan, Christopher Morris, Bob Muhlnickel, Mark Murphy, John Oberdiek, Govind Persad, George Rainbolt, Massimo Renzo, Connie Rosati, David Schmidtz, Russ Shafer-Landau, Steve Sverdlik, Victor Tadros, Brian Tamanaha, Francois Tanguay-Renaud, Patrick Tomlin, Justin Tosi, Andrew Valls, Jerry Vildostegui, Bas van der Vossen, Alec Walen, Carl Wellman, and Ekow Yankah.

Several of these folks were especially influential. I began working on punishment when David Schmidtz invited me to present an essay at the Arizona Current Research Workshop. This essay naively presumed the truth of rights forfeiture theory, so I got much more interested in the topic when Zach Hoskins politely called my attention to the fact that virtually no one takes this approach seriously. The Earhart Foundation offered me a fellowship to work on this topic, and I soon began attending conferences (many of which were organized by Antony Duff and Sandra Marshall) on criminal law. Although my views depart radically from his, I gained an enormous amount by grappling with Duff's peerless writing on the subject. Those who work in the area know how busy Antony is, but he somehow made the time to write me copious insightful notes on the many drafts I shamelessly sent him. Indeed, were it not for the reassuring replies that John Simmons (a fellow forfeiture theorist) offered in response to my countless panicked emails, I suspect that Antony's forceful objections would have led me to abandon this project. Finally, once I had completed a draft of the book, Patrick Tomlin very kindly organized a manuscript workshop at the University of Reading. I took quite a beating on that day, but I am profoundly grateful to Patrick and his compatriots for making it abundantly clear where my views would encounter the most resistance.

This book draws upon some of my previously published work. Chapters 1, 2, and 6 draw upon "The Rights Forfeiture Theory of Punishment," which was published in *Ethics*; chapter 3 draws upon "Rights and State Punishment," which appeared in the *Journal of Philosophy*; chapter 5 draws upon "Procedural Rights," which was published in *Legal Theory*; and chapter 7 draws upon "Rights Forfeiture and Mala Prohibita," which appeared in *The Constitution of Criminal Law*. (Complete bibliographic information for these articles can be found in the references.) I am happy to thank *Ethics*, the

Journal of Philosophy, Legal Theory, and Oxford University Press for allowing me to draw on this work.

It has once again been a delight to work with Peter Ohlin and his staff at Oxford University Press. Lucy Randall, Andrew Ward, and their associates there make the production process as painless as possible.

As always, my greatest debts are the most personal. Above all, I am so grateful for Donna's love and patience as my grumpiness escalated over the much longer-than-anticipated time it took me to complete this project.

Chapter 1

Introduction

This book argues that those of us concerned with the moral permissibility of punishment should shift our focus from general justifying aims to moral side constraints. In my view, the traditional approaches to punishment help explain why we may *want* to punish, but none can establish the permissibility of doing so.[1] If we seek to explain the permissibility of punishment, only the rights forfeiture theory will suffice.

THE INADEQUACY OF THE TRADITIONAL APPROACHES

For the purposes of this book, I adopt Douglas Husak's definition of punishment: "a response amounts to a punishment when it deliberately imposes a stigmatizing deprivation or hardship. A treatment is not punitive because it *happens* to deprive or stigmatize. The very *purpose* of a response must be to deprive and to stigmatize before it qualifies as a punishment. That is, punishments *intentionally* impose a stigmatizing deprivation."[2]

We should not lose sight of the fact that punishment intentionally stigmatizes, but I would like to begin by emphasizing that punishment necessarily involves visiting hard treatment upon those who are punished. Given that persons typically have a moral right not to be subjected to this hard treatment, it would seem natural to conclude that the permissibility of punishment is centrally a question of rights. This insight appears lost on the vast majority of theorists working on punishment who focus instead on the *aims* of punishment. According to retributivism, the general justifying aim of punishment is to serve justice by giving wrongdoers the hard treatment they deserve; utilitarianism suggests that the aim is to produce better consequences (chiefly by deterring everyone from committing crimes); moral education theory insists that the aim is to help morally educate the wrongdoer and society at large; expressivist theory claims that the central aim is for society to express its emphatic denunciation of the wrongdoer; restitutive theory alleges that the aim is to restore the victims; and societal safety-valve theory claims that the aim is to provide a peaceful outlet for socially disruptive emotions. I think that all of these aims help explain why we should *want* a properly constructed system of punishment, but none shows why it would be permissible to institute one. Only a rights-based analysis will suffice here, because the type of justification we seek for punishment must demonstrate that punishment is permissible, and it would be permissible only if it violated no one's rights.

To appreciate this basic point about the relationship between aims, rights, and adequate justification, imagine that I want some of Bill Gates's money in order to fund release time from my professorial responsibilities, so that I can dedicate myself full-time to designing a new type of mosquito-repellent clothing that would better protect people from the Zika virus. These admirable aims may well explain why I *want* some of Gates's money, but they cannot by themselves explain why I would be *justified* in taking it, because they say nothing about the various *rights* involved. Absent some sort of explanation to the contrary, Gates stands in a privileged position of ownership over his money, and this position entails that I may not unilaterally help myself to it, no matter how laudable my aims are. If Gates had promised to finance my venture, then this may well explain why I may permissibly help myself to the funds in question, but in this case Gates's promise rather than my aims are the crucial variable. And certainly one can imagine a scenario in which Gates agrees to finance my project precisely because I have such lofty and important aims, but even here my aims are not by themselves a sufficient justification. Without Gates's consent, I may not permissibly take his money. In light of this, the centrality of rights (and the inadequacy of aims) is apparent.

Because being punished appears to violate one's life, liberty, and/or property rights, the permissibility of punishment seems to hinge on whether punishment is compatible with these rights. After all, just as the fact that Gates owns his money entails that others may not permissibly commandeer it, each individual's privileged position of moral dominion over her own affairs entails that others may not permissibly incarcerate or otherwise punish her. However, just as Gates can waive his right to his money (if he gives it to me, for instance), one can forfeit one's right against being punished. When one wrongly harms another, for example, one forfeits the privileged position of dominion over one's self-regarding affairs. Moreover, how harshly one may be punished depends on how badly one mistreats others. This is why the innocent may not permissibly be punished, those who commit minor wrongs may be punished only a correspondingly small amount, and those who behave worse may be punished more severely. As W. D. Ross puts it:

> the offender, by violating the life or liberty or property of another, has lost his own right to have his life, liberty, or property respected, so that the state has no *prima facie* duty to spare him, as it has a *prima facie* duty to spare the innocent. It is morally at liberty to injure him as he has injured others, or to inflict any lesser injury on him, or to spare him, exactly as consideration

> both of the good of the community and of his own good requires. If, on the other hand, a man has respected the rights of others, there is a strong and distinctive objection to the state's inflicting any penalty on him with a view to the good of the community or even to his own good.[3]

Thus, contrary to the traditional strategy of citing the valuable aims that punishment can realize, the best approach for those who seek to explain the permissibility of punishment would seem to be to focus on how wrongdoers have forfeited their rights against hard treatment.

Rights forfeiture theory can be endorsed in either a strong or a weak form. Advocates of the more modest interpretation insist that forfeiture alone is insufficient; in order to be permissible, punishment must also promote some important (deterrent, retributive, or other) aim. Defenders of this weak version do not deny that punishment is permissible only when it is necessary to advance some valuable aim; they merely emphasize that realizing these aims would not suffice to justify punishment if the person punished had not forfeited her right. More ambitious forfeiture theorists, however, suggest that the forfeiture is necessary and sufficient. According to this more radical view, one may permissibly punish anyone who has forfeited her rights *even if this hard treatment will not serve any important purpose.* In other words, the weak version regards rights forfeiture as a necessary *supplement* to the more traditional theories, whereas the strong interpretation views forfeiture as a *substitute.*

Many theorists find the weak version more palatable, but I favor the stronger, more controversial position. I appreciate that securing important goods would be necessary to explain why a moral right has been *overridden,* but I believe that no such benefits need to be cited when a right has been forfeited precisely because, once a right has been forfeited, it ceases to exist and thus need not be defeated. I therefore recommend that we concentrate on which rights wrongdoers forfeit, because this forfeiture strikes me as both necessary and sufficient to explain the permissibility of punishment.[4]

MY UNDERSTANDING OF MORAL RIGHTS

Those who deny the existence of moral rights are unlikely to be impressed with my approach to punishment. Even those who believe in rights may understand them differently than I, though, so it is worth taking some time at the outset to make plain how I conceive of moral rights and their corresponding duties.

In my quieter moments, I worry that several of these claims need to be qualified, but for the purposes of this book I am happy to claim allegiance to the following: With the exception of nonidentity cases, I believe that all moral duties correspond to correlative moral rights; what many characterize as imperfect duties—like the putative duty of charity—I would analyze in aretaic rather than deontic terms. I do not think any moral rights are inalienable or absolute; in my view, all rights can be waived, all rights can be forfeited, and all rights are vulnerable to being overridden. When a right is either waived or forfeited, it ceases to exist. As a consequence, when a second party acts in a way that would have transgressed this right (had it continued to exist), she does not owe anything to the person who waived or forfeited the right. An overridden right, however, continues to exist, and thus a second party who permissibly infringes upon an overridden right may owe restitution, compensation, and/or an apology to the right-holder. I believe that all rights may be proportionately enforced.[5] I think that there are positive moral rights; in particular, if someone is sufficiently imperiled and you can rescue her at no unreasonable cost to yourself, I believe that she has a right that you save her even in the absence of any previous transaction or preexisting relationship between the two of you.

I believe that there are preinstitutional moral rights, including the right not to be punished. While this right (like every right) is vulnerable to being overridden in extraordinary circumstances, this right explains why it is generally impermissible to punish an innocent person. One can forfeit the right not to be punished, but one does not forfeit a right unless one culpably violates (or at least attempts to violate) someone else's right. One necessarily loses one's moral immunity to (proportionate) punishment whenever one culpably violates a moral right. Finally, I believe that the right to punish is competitive; in other words, *anyone* (i.e., not only the person whose right was violated) may permissibly punish a wrongdoer.

To get a sense of the implications of these beliefs, notice how I would analyze the following scenarios. First, imagine that I am lounging beside the pool when I see an unattended infant crawl into the pool. There is no one else around, and this young child will clearly drown unless I retrieve her. Everyone agrees that I would merit some type of moral criticism if I failed to save her, but theorists disagree about whether I have a *duty* to do so. While authors like Peter Singer insist that I have a duty of justice to save this baby, others allege that my failure to help would merely be suberogatory.[6] Jeffrie Murphy, for instance, argues that

> I can be morally lacking even in cases in which I violate no one's rights. For example: I am sitting in a lounge chair next to a swimming pool. A child (not mine) is drowning in the pool a few inches from where I am sitting. I notice him and realize that all I have to do to save him is put down my drink, reach down, grab him by the trunks, and pull him out (he is so light I could do it with one hand without even getting out of my seat). If I do not save him I violate no rights (strangers do not have a right to be saved by me) but would still reveal myself as a piece of moral slime properly to be shunned by all decent people.[7]

I follow Murphy in thinking that one can be morally lacking without violating rights, but I deny that samaritan rescues fall in this category. If I am waiting to pay at the grocery store with a cart full of items when a woman holding only a box of children's medicine and two screaming infants gets in line behind me, for instance, I leave myself open to moral criticism if I do not offer her the opportunity to go before me, even though I would be squarely within my rights to insist on checking out first. In my view, while it would be merely suberogatory for me to fail to invite the harried mother to go before me in line at the grocery store, I would act impermissibly if I failed to rescue someone (like the drowning baby) who was sufficiently imperiled when I could do so at no unreasonable cost.

But given that I morally ought to allow the distressed mother to check out before me, and I morally ought to save the drowning baby, why distinguish between actions that are required by duty and those which are merely suberogatory? As indicated above, I believe that there are a number of important implications that follow from having a moral duty. First, each genuine moral duty corresponds to someone else's correlative moral right. Thus, when I allege that I have a moral duty to save the drowning infant but no duty to allow the distressed shopper to skip ahead of me in line, this entails that the drowning infant has a right that I save her but that the shopper has no right to check out before me. Second, following Joel Feinberg, I believe that, while others may urge, exhort, and encourage me not to behave in a suberogatory fashion, no one is in the normatively privileged position to demand that I do so.[8] Because a right-holder is morally entitled to claim performance of the corresponding duty, though, she is morally empowered to insist that she receive her due. Thus, while the weary shopper may politely ask me if I would allow her to move ahead of me, she cannot claim the spot before me in the same way that a drowning person (whom I could save at no unreasonable cost) may demand that I save her. Third, I believe that all rights may be coercively enforced by the right-holder and (typically, at least) third parties. As a consequence, while neither the weary shopper nor any third party may force me to move aside in the checkout line, a drowning person (or a third party) would be morally permitted to (proportionately) coerce me to perform the samaritan rescue. Finally, I believe all and only those who culpably fail to do their duties forfeit their rights against proportionate punishment. Thus, while I would forfeit no rights if I failed to allow the distressed shopper to go ahead of me, I would lose my moral immunity to punishment if I failed to rescue the drowning baby.

Putting all of the above together, I would say the following about the moral relations in a situation like a drowning person whom I might save without unreasonable cost to myself. First of all, I have no moral discretion: I am morally required to save her. Second, the drowning person has a moral right that I save her, and if I fail to do so, I violate that right. Third, if there was another person beside the pool who for some reason was unable to save the drowning person (perhaps she is paralyzed and so cannot swim) but would be able to coerce me (suppose that she has a gun), this third party would be justified in coercing me to perform the rescue. And finally, if I did fail to save the drowning child, I would forfeit my right against being (proportionately) punished.

Finally, I mark the difference between suberogatory acts versus those that violate the rights of others by distinguishing sharply between "deplorable" and "culpable." As I use these terms, one behaves *deplorably* when one does not offer to let the weary mother with sick infants check out before one at the grocery store, but one is not *culpable* unless one violates someone else's right. Not everyone understands "deplorable" and "culpable" to have these distinct meanings (and as Murphy's analysis of the drowning child illustrates, there is room to disagree about which particular acts violate the rights of others), but it is common to insist that not everyone who is morally lacking is liable to punishment. As Alec Walen notes, "liberals think such matters of virtue and vice (or sin) are best left to the autonomous individual, and are not proper bases of punishment."[9] The central thesis of this book is that there is a weighty moral side constraint against punishing even the most deplorable people unless they have culpably violated (or at least attempted to violate) someone's rights.

FORFEITURE THEORY AND ITS IMPLICATIONS

Before summarizing the chapters to follow, I should stress that this book provides neither a complete account of punishment nor an exhaustive theory of criminal law. More minimally, it seeks only to articulate and defend a particular version of forfeiture theory, and then to explore some of its most striking implications for criminal law.

It is not terribly controversial to claim that forfeiture is necessary for the permissibility of punishment, but there is widespread and deep-seated resistance to the more ambitious thesis that forfeiture is necessary *and sufficient* for the permissibility of punishment. Chapter 2 defends this strong version of rights forfeiture theory against a variety of apparently fatal objections, including the concern that it licenses gratuitous acts of punishment.

Even if we agree that punishment is permissible just in case the person punished has forfeited her right against this hard treatment, it remains an open question *who* may mete out the punishment. If anyone has an exclusive right to punish the wrongdoer, it would presumably be the victim, so those of us inclined to think that the state enjoys sole authority over the punitive process must explain how the state acquires its moral dominion over the criminal legal proceedings. Chapter 3 provides this explanation by arguing that the state violates no rights in claiming a monopoly over the punitive process only because it is uniquely capable of adequately realizing the morally significant aims that a system of punishment can achieve. A state is legitimate, in my view, just in case it satisfactorily protects the human rights of all of its constituents, and a state could not successfully perform this crucial function unless it enjoyed exclusive authority to punish all wrongdoers within its territorial jurisdiction.

The standard way to distinguish between torts and crimes is to allege that the latter are in some important sense distinctively "public." I think we must look elsewhere for a principled distinction, and in chapter 4 I argue that the crucial difference between tort and criminal law ought to map onto the distinction between rights infringements and rights violations. I contend that moral rights are central to both areas of law but that tort law is an appropriate response to rights-related harms, whereas criminal law is a fitting response to rights-related culpability.

Chapter 5 explores whether a wrongdoer forfeits her right against being punished as soon as she violates someone else's rights or only after she has been duly convicted of doing so. Governments unquestionably have pressing reasons to design their criminal legal institutions carefully so that no citizen is vulnerable to being wrongly punished, overpunished, or otherwise harassed by government officials, but I argue that these reasons are wholly instrumental. I thus conclude that there are no preinstitutional procedural rights, not even a right against being punished without first being found guilty by a fair and reliable process.

Chapter 6 is the most vexing (and tentative) portion of the book. Here I grapple with the problem of relatedness, which requires me to confront foundational questions in moral theory and their implications for forfeiture theory. The core issue is whether a wrongdoer forfeits her right against being harmed for any reason whatsoever (the unlimited-reasons approach) or only for reasons appropriately related to the wrongdoing (the limited-reasons approach). After rebutting the initial impression that the unlimited-reasons approach is wholly implausible, I offer some reasons in defense of the conclusion that wrongdoers do not forfeit their rights against being *harmed* in general; more specifically, they forfeit their right against being *punished*, which (by definition) involves being intentionally stigmatized for one's putative wrongdoing.

Mala prohibita crimes raise difficult questions for forfeiture theorists who believe that one does not forfeit any rights unless one violates a right because, unlike in the case of *mala in se* crimes, it is not obvious whose right the *mala prohibita* criminal violates. Compare, for instance, the *mala in se* crime of driving while intoxicated to the *mala prohibita* crime of driving on a public road without a valid vehicle registration sticker displayed in the legally required spot on one's front windshield. It seems clear that inebriated drivers violate the rights of others by exposing them to unacceptable risks, but whose right is violated by one's failure to display a vehicle registration sticker on one's car? The discussion of chapter 7 explains that *mala prohibita* criminals can sometimes be permissibly punished because one's fellow citizens have a right that one obey the just laws of a legitimate state.

The book concludes by assessing the current US criminal legal system. When we evaluate the status quo through the lens of moral side constraints rather than in terms of general justifying aims, it becomes clear that we are not merely doing a poor job of achieving valuable goods; we are violating basic moral rights on a massive scale. Given our utterly indefensible practices of overcriminalizing, overpunishing, incarcerating inmates in inhumane prison conditions, and doing all of this against a backdrop of systemic injustice, it is no exaggeration to condemn the status quo as a widespread and systematic human rights atrocity.

Chapter 2

Defending Forfeiture Theory

Whereas weak rights forfeiture theory alleges only that forfeiture is necessary for the permissibility of punishment, the strong version insists that forfeiture is necessary and sufficient. Critics contend that neither version is satisfactory, because the weak version does not offer an alternative to the traditional approaches, and the strong version is beset with insuperable difficulties. The weak version of forfeiture theory does not fully depart from the traditional theories because, in denying that forfeiture is sufficient to justify punishment, it concedes that we must still invoke a general justifying aim in order to explain the permissibility of punishment. The strong version offers a genuine alternative, but many regard it as untenable. This chapter defends the strong version of rights forfeiture theory against a variety of potential objections, including the concern that it licenses gratuitous acts of punishment.

STRONG RIGHTS FORFEITURE THEORY AND GRATUITOUS PUNISHMENT

It is not terribly controversial to claim that rights forfeiture is necessary for the permissibility of punishment, but most strenuously resist the strong rights forfeiture thesis that it is also sufficient. After all, if forfeiture is sufficient to justify punishment, it would be permissible to punish those who have forfeited their rights *even if no good came of it*. But given the suffering associated with punishment, it seems barbarous to allege that we may permissibly punish someone in the absence of compelling moral reasons to do so. Advocates of the traditional approaches to punishment thus resist my plea to shift our focus from aims to side constraints because they regard these aims as necessary to justify the suffering imposed on those who are punished. We are right to dedicate so much attention to general justifying aims, according to this line of thinking, because any theory that permitted punishment even if no deterrent, retributive, restitutive, communicative, or other good was thereby achieved would be reprehensible.

I acknowledge that these traditional goals help explain why we should want to punish, and (as I will emphasize in the next two chapters) I believe that we could not justify the institution of *state* punishment unless the criminal legal system performed vitally important tasks, but I deny that a single act of punishment must produce (or even be expected to produce) any good in order for it to be permissible. Again, given the suffering typically involved in punishment, many find this view implausible. When Victor Tadros discovered that I endorsed strong rights forfeiture theory, for instance, he boomed, "I never knew you were such a sadist!"[1] I do not have much of an appetite for sadism, but there is a kernel of truth in Tadros's quip, because I do believe that even very extreme forms of sadism can be morally permissible.

Before discussing sadism and arguing for the permissibility of gratuitous punishment, it is important to stress that one can defend the permissibility of something without necessarily applauding it. Consider divorce, for instance. My own view is that many married couples (especially couples with children) are far too quick to divorce. Divorce is undeniably the best option in some cases, but in many instances I think that all involved would be better off in the long run if folks were more committed to staying together through the tough times. Despite harboring this old-fashioned view, I do not question the moral permissibility of divorce. And crucially, even when I believe that any given couple should stick together, I have no doubt that the married individuals enjoy the right to decide whether or not to divorce. (And I certainly deny that third parties may force married couples to stay together.) As this example illustrates, there is nothing contradictory or otherwise problematic about defending the permissibility of X without recommending X as in any way rational or laudable, and so my case for the permissibility of sadism need not imply that I applaud sadism in any shape or form.

With this in mind, let us consider two actual cases of sadism: the first quite mild and the second terribly extreme. The first instance features my mother-in-law, Betty, and the second involves Armin Meiwes. When I first met Betty (who was not then but is now my mother-in-law), I was wearing a pair of tennis shoes that I would sometimes, but not always, tie. On the day I met Betty, my shoes happened to be untied. For reasons that remain unclear to me, this irritated Betty. (Indeed, over twenty years have passed since we first met, and Betty still occasionally mentions how much it bothered her that I would sometimes leave my shoes untied.) I was virtually indifferent to whether these shoes were tied or not (which is why I sometimes tied them and other times did not), so it would not have been a great sacrifice for me to tie them whenever I was in Betty's presence. But I must confess that I did not. Indeed, I often deliberately left my shoes untied when I would see Betty precisely because I knew that it would bother her. Put plainly, I took a small bit of joy in provoking her in this way.

What should we say of my behavior in this case? Should I be proud or ashamed of my conduct? And were my actions permissible? I do not allege that I was the model of virtue and maturity. If I had been nicer and more mature, I would have made sure to tie my shoes whenever I was in Betty's company. After all, I did not care nearly as much as Betty whether my shoes were tied. Even if my actions were unkind and immature, though, I think that they were permissible. I say this because I believe that (1) one acts permissibly as long as one acts within one's rights, (2) one's rights are bounded by the rights of others, and (3) those acting within their rights may permissibly act for any reasons whatsoever. Applying these claims to the case at hand, I believe that I am generally at liberty to either tie or not tie my shoes precisely because no one else has a right that I tie them. This bilateral liberty is vulnerable to being overridden (as it might be if some disaster would occur if I left my shoes untied, for instance), but I do not believe that Betty had a claim right that I tie my shoes merely because she cared so much more about this than I.[2] And given that I was squarely within my rights to leave my shoes untied in Betty's presence, I was morally free to do so even if no good would come of it, including if I was motivated only by the sadistic pleasure I sought to derive from irritating my girlfriend's mother. In sum, I think this particular case of (mild) sadism is an example of my acting viciously but permissibly.

Even if one agrees with my analysis of this case, one might question its relevance to punishment. Because punishment involves hard treatment, the stakes are considerably higher for this level of suffering. Most important, while others have no right that I tie my shoes, everyone does enjoy a right against being punished, and this right might entail that one may not permissibly be made to suffer unless some compensating good would come of it. This is a legitimate point, so let us now consider a much more extreme example of sadism, the case of Armin Meiwes and Bernd Jurgen Armando Brandes. As I understand the facts, Brandes responded to Meiwes's online solicitation for someone who wanted to be slaughtered and killed. Meiwes and Brandes got together and indulged in a variety of sadomasochistic acts (including cutting off, cooking, and trying to eat Brandes's penis) before Meiwes finally killed and ate Brandes. All of the evidence indicates that Brandes consented every step along the way, and that Meiwes would have refrained from all of these sadistic acts if Brandes had at any point withdrawn his consent.

What should we say of Meiwes in this case? Should Meiwes be proud or ashamed of his behavior? And were Meiwes's actions permissible? I concede that Meiwes's character leaves a great deal to be desired. Insofar as he valued his own sadistic thrills over another person's life, Meiwes displayed deplorable values. Even so, if we abstract away from all issues having to do with special obligations (if we assume for the sake of argument that German law did not criminally prohibit consensual killing, that Brandes had no dependents to whom he had a duty to continue living, and that Meiwes had not promised anyone he would refrain from these types of acts, for instance), I believe that Meiwes acted permissibly. I recognize that Brandes had a right to life and that this right would ordinarily make it impermissible for anyone to kill him, but I believe that Brandes enjoyed broad moral discretion over his self-regarding affairs, a discretion that entitled him to waive his right against Meiwes's killing him. And if Brandes gave his free and informed consent to all of Meiwes's actions, Meiwes acted permissibly even though he deliberately killed another human being merely to indulge his sadistic urges.[3] As I see it, the same reasoning I invoked in the shoe-tying case applies here as well. Meiwes acted permissibly as long as he acted within his rights, and he acted within his rights in this case because (even though killing Brandes would ordinarily violate Brandes's right to life) Brandes explicitly waived this right.

Not everyone will be comfortable with this analysis. Most obviously, some might question whether we really enjoy such broad moral dominion over our self-regarding affairs. *Volenti non fit injuria* is widely accepted (few doubt our ability to waive our rights against being grabbed when we consent to a wrestling match, for instance), but this does not mean that we necessarily have complete discretion over our self-regarding affairs, so that we can waive all of our rights, including the right to life.[4] One way to motivate this thought is to allege that the same feature of others that gives rise to our duty to respect them (their autonomous, rational nature, perhaps) also generates duties regarding ourselves. (After all, our nature is no less autonomous and rational.)[5] Our dominion over our self-regarding affairs is thus limited, according to this view, because we are *stewards*, rather than owners, of our lives. If we all owned ourselves, then Brandes was at liberty to discard his life just as he might dispose of a table, or any other inanimate possession. But Brandes's life was not Brandes's to discard; because of its unconditional value, Brandes had a duty to respect his own life, even when disrespecting it would not harm anyone else.

One would expect Kantians to be especially attracted to this type of account, so it is noteworthy that Thomas E. Hill, Jr., a leading Kantian, shies away from characterizing the moral values involved in terms of duties. As he explains in "Self-Regarding Suicide,"

> One might hold, for example, that suicide *from certain attitudes* is always, or nearly always, objectionable, at least a falling short of a moral ideal, and that this is not solely because it is contrary to the welfare or rights of others. This would allow that some suicides are justified and even commendable, but suicides rooted in certain attitudes (for example, undervaluation of rational, autonomous human life) would be opposed. They would be opposed, not strictly condemned as immoral; and they would be opposed as out of line with an ideal moral attitude toward one's life, not as a violation of a strict duty to oneself.[6]

Given his Kantian inclinations, I am not sure why Hill is at such pains to stress that our moral concerns about (some) suicides should not be cashed out in terms of duties, but I can say that I favor this approach because I reserve talk of duties and correlative rights for the domain of justice, which I conceive as the realm of potential conflict adjudication. There is obviously much more to morality than adjudicating potential conflicts, and my refusal to explicate these other domains in terms of rights and duties is not meant to indicate that these realms are somehow less important.[7] I restrict talk of rights and duties to the language of conflict adjudication because doing so best captures the distinctive nature and function of duties and rights.[8] So, whatever Hill's motivation for avoiding talk of a self-regarding duty not to commit suicide, I analyze this case in aretaic rather than deontic terms because I believe that all duties are owed to a specific party, and I am uncomfortable with the notion of someone owing a duty to herself.[9] Like Hill, I believe that there is ample room to morally criticize someone who insufficiently values her own life, but I deny that anyone has a *duty* to appropriately value her own life (and I deny that others may forcibly interfere when one exhibits insufficient concern for one's own well-being).

If all of this is true, then we need not retreat from the thesis that Brandes enjoyed a privileged position of moral dominion over his self-regarding affairs that enabled him to waive his right to life, thereby making it permissible for Meiwes to kill him. And if we can waive our rights (including our right to life), then why can we not equally forfeit all of our rights? With this in mind, consider a forfeiture analogue of the present case. Instead of inflicting pain only on those who explicitly waive their rights against this suffering, suppose that Meiwes is a sadist (like those Nozick imagines in *Anarchy, State and Utopia*) who metes out hard treatment exclusively against those who have forfeited their rights.[10] Specifically, imagine that Meiwes tortures and kills Brandes only after Brandes has forfeited his rights against this hard treatment by committing some unspeakably heinous crime. Again, I am happy to grant that Meiwes's sadism is a pronounced character flaw, but it does not follow from this that his punishment of Brandes is necessarily impermissible. If Meiwes's sadism is permissible when Brandes has waived his right against these gruesome acts, why should we be any less confident that Meiwes's sadism is permissible when Brandes has forfeited his right against this punishment?

Those who remain reluctant to embrace this reasoning have several potential responses: (1) they can argue that at least some rights cannot be waived, (2) they might insist that forfeiture operates differently than waiving, or (3) they can allege that gratuitously harming someone can be impermissible even when it violates no rights. Consider each potential response in turn.

First, because a wholesale rejection of the *volenti* principle seems implausible (few would deny that most sexual acts are permissible just in case the parties involved consent to them, for instance), a more promising approach would be to argue that a few select rights (including perhaps the rights against being killed, tortured, and enslaved) are inalienable. As I indicated above, I am not optimistic that this position can be vindicated. Even if this view can be satisfactorily defended, though, it would not necessarily defeat strong rights forfeiture theory; at most, it would suggest that there are limits on which rights can be forfeited. If we can waive most but not all of our rights, then the parallel position would seem to be that we can forfeit most but not all of our rights. If we can waive all but our right to life, for instance, then the natural conclusion would not seem to be that we can forfeit our right to life and yet this forfeiture fails to make it permissible for someone else to kill us unless some good would come of it; at most, the appropriate conclusion to draw would seem to be that we cannot forfeit our right to life.[11] If our dominion over our self-regarding affairs is restricted so as to render us unable to waive some of our rights, then perhaps these limits on our dominion equally entail that we cannot forfeit our inalienable rights. Thus, even if limits on our self-ownership could somehow be conclusively established, this would only potentially restrict the scope, rather than undermine the plausibility, of strong rights forfeiture theory.

A second strategy would be to distinguish sharply between waiving and forfeiting rights. In particular, one might allege that, unlike waiving, forfeiture has a necessity condition built into it, so that one does not forfeit one's right against punishment unless this punishment is necessary to secure some important good.[12] Other things being equal, one would presume that waivers and forfeitures function similarly, but recent work on the morality of defensive force indicates that distinguishing between the two in this way need not be merely ad hoc. Consider the work of Jeff McMahan, for instance, the leading ethicist who analyzes the permissibility of defensive force in terms of forfeiture. In *Killing in War,* McMahan suggests that necessity and proportionality are internal to liability, so that an unjust combatant would not be liable to defensive force if this force was either disproportionately or unnecessarily harmful. Given that I believe that wrongdoers forfeit their right against only a proportionate punishment, perhaps I should follow McMahan's lead and claim also that wrongdoers forfeit their rights only against punishment that is necessary to serve some valuable aim.

I resist this move for two reasons. First of all, while I agree with much of McMahan's critique of traditional just war theory, I am not sure that the ethics of defensive force can be explained principally in terms of forfeiture. But even if we assume that McMahan's analysis of defensive force is entirely correct, I would be inclined to distinguish sharply between forfeiture against defensive force and forfeiture against punishment. Admittedly, we would pretheoretically expect the various kinds of forfeiture to mirror one another, but it is worth noting that McMahan himself understands these two types of forfeiture to operate very differently. Not only does he allege that culpability is required for forfeiture against punishment but not for forfeiture against defensive attack, he stresses that there is no necessity condition when harm is deserved. As he explains:

> In war, the goal for which people may be liable to be harmed is usually defensive: to prevent the achievement of an unjust cause, and to defend people from harms that would otherwise be inflicted by unjust combatants in their efforts to achieve an unjust cause. Because people can be liable to harm only in relation to a goal of this sort, the assignment of liability is governed by a requirement of necessity. If harming a person is unnecessary for the achievement of the relevant type of goal, that person cannot be liable to be harmed. The infliction of deserved harm is, by contrast, not governed by a requirement of necessity, since the value of a person's getting what he deserves is not instrumental and hence is not necessary for anything beyond itself.[13]

I do not mean to suggest that McMahan is an unqualified ally here, because he is not. By invoking desert, McMahan incorporates a retributive aim that is lacking from my view.[14] Even so, the fact that he understands the moral vulnerability to punishment to be so different from liability to defensive force shows that we need not worry that my account of forfeiture with respect to punishment differs from McMahan's theory of forfeiture with respect to defensive force *even if we assume that the latter is entirely correct.*

A third potential response to my defense of the permissibility of sadism would be to question my restricted use of the term "duty." If one denies that duties necessarily correspond to the rights of others, one might insist that an agent can act contrary to duty *even when she wrongs no one*. And if an agent can have duties to refrain from acts that violate no rights, we cannot assume that acts that cause gratuitous suffering are merely suberogatory as long as they are committed exclusively against people who have either waived or forfeited their rights. Put in terms of my earlier example, perhaps Meiwes acted wrongly when he tortured and killed Brandes, *even though Brandes waived his rights against these acts* because there is an impersonal duty against sadism (or more plausibly, I think, a duty against committing sufficiently harmful sadistic acts).

Insofar as it questions the manner in which I distinguish between deontic and aretaic ethics, this third potential reply presents the most sweeping and fundamental challenge to my approach. And we may now be at an impasse, because if this there is an impersonal duty not to cause gratuitous suffering, punishment would be impermissible unless it achieves some worthwhile aim *even when a right has been forfeited*.

In part because I think there are good reasons to be skeptical of impersonal duties, but also because—as I will show in subsequent chapters—retreating from strong to weak rights forfeiture theory has no implications for criminal legal institutions in a legitimate state, this potential impasse does not alarm me. Even so, I would like to offer one last consideration in favor of the idea that there are virtue-making, rather than duty-imposing, moral reasons to refrain from gratuitously harming others. In particular, consider my decision to buy a copy of Tadros's *The Ends of Harm* when I could have done more good by checking the book out of the library and donating the money I saved to charity. Perhaps Peter Singer would allege that I had a duty to give the funds in question to charity, but I subscribe the commonsense view that it was permissible for me to purchase Tadros's book even though there were clearly virtue-making moral reasons in favor of my giving the money to charity. But if I acted permissibly in buying the book even though I could have easily reduced the amount of suffering in the world, why are we so sure that Meiwes necessarily acted impermissibly when he chose to increase the amount of suffering in the world? Meiwes and I each acted in a way that resulted in there being greater net suffering, but neither of us violated any rights. And given that I acted permissibly (but less than virtuously) by indulging my desire for Tadros's book, why not similarly say that Meiwes acted permissibly (but viciously) by indulging his sadistic desires?

Here a persistent critic faces a crossroads: She can either lean heavily on the distinction between causing and alleviating suffering, or she can join consequentialists who suppose that there is an impersonal duty to maximally reduce net suffering. The latter option amounts to a wholesale rejection of the commonsensical notion of moral rights, though, and the former requires the critic of strong forfeiture theory (1) to argue for the existence of impersonal duties, (2) to argue that the mandate to refrain from causing gratuitous suffering is among these impersonal duties, and (3) to argue that the distinction between doing and allowing is so important that we can have impersonal duties to avoid causing gratuitous harm without having impersonal duties to prevent comparable harms. I do not know the literature on these various questions well enough to pronounce that this burden has not, and cannot, be met, but I am pessimistic that these arguments can be successfully made. Those who are more optimistic than I, though, have a road map for their critique of strong rights forfeiture theory.

To review what has been a long and convoluted discussion: Because there is ample room both to morally criticize those who gratuitously harm others even when they act permissibly, and to distinguish the institutional question of what justifies state punishment from the interactional question of when an individual punishment may be permissible, I contend that there is nothing implausible about the strong rights forfeiture view, even though it admittedly allows for the permissibility of gratuitous punishments. To be clear: I concede that *state* punishment would not be justified unless the criminal legal system secured vitally important goods that would be unavailable in its absence, and that someone who punished a person merely to scratch a sadistic itch would be acting deplorably. Even so, I believe that a punishment that serves no other purpose might nonetheless be morally permissible. Just as a sadistic act that would otherwise violate someone's right might become permissible when the person has waived her right against this treatment, a particular gratuitous punishment that would otherwise violate someone's rights might become permissible when the person being made to suffer has forfeited her rights against this hard treatment.

Even if strong rights forfeiture theory should not be rejected because of its implications regarding the permissibility of gratuitous harm, it faces a number of other apparently devastating objections. The standard objections include the problem of justification; the problem of status; the problem of indeterminate authorization; the problem of suitability; the problem of duration and breadth; and the problem of rights type.[15] As I argue below, though, none of these standard objections is compelling.

THE PROBLEM OF JUSTIFICATION AND THE PROBLEM OF STATUS

The problem of justification alleges that defenders of forfeiture theory have yet to provide a satisfactory argument for the claim that wrongdoers forfeit their rights. Alan Goldman, Christopher Morris, and John Simmons all offer, or at least gesture toward, arguments on behalf of rights forfeiture. Goldman suggests that rights forfeiture might follow from the relationship between rights and duties; Morris proposes a contractarian explanation; and Simmons invokes fairness.[16] If any of these arguments is successful, then the problem is solved. Theorists like David Boonin, however, have found these arguments wanting.[17] For the sake of argument, let us suppose that Boonin is correct. If so, I must either generate my own argument or concede that I am merely asserting that wrongdoers forfeit their rights.

I must confess that I have no original argument, and thus must assume the truth of this central claim. All arguments have to start somewhere, though, and given that there is no other considered conviction regarding punishment about which I am more confident (I am at least as confident that rights can be forfeited as I am in any of the assumptions Goldman, Morris, and Simmons make in order to argue for the conclusion of rights forfeiture, for instance), this seems like a promising place to start.[18] To appreciate why I adopt this strategy, it is worth contrasting my approach with one of the most important recent contributions to the literature on punishment, Victor Tadros's duty view.[19]

While Tadros does not advertise it as such (indeed, forfeiture is not even listed in the index of *The Ends of Harm*), I regard his approach as a type of rights forfeiture theory. As I read his work, Tadros recognizes the instrumental value of punishment but denies that the hard treatment of punishment can be justified solely in terms of the good consequences it brings. Instead, Tadros posits that wrongdoers incur enforceable remedial duties to protect their victims against further wrongdoing. Tadros then offers a series of ingenious arguments to show that this secondary duty explains how wrongdoers come to lack the right against punishment that they previously enjoyed. Let us assume that all of these arguments work. If so, Tadros has produced a sophisticated rights forfeiture account that begins with a (modest and plausible) premise about the acquisition of a secondary duty that is incurred when a primary duty is violated, and then leads to the conclusion that wrongdoers have forfeited their rights against punishment. One important attraction of Tadros's theory, then, is that it provides an argument—rather than merely assumes—that wrongdoers forfeit rights.

Given the plausibility of the idea that wrongdoers can acquire remedial duties when they breach primary duties, Tadros's account strikes me as quite promising. For two reasons, though, I do not see this approach as providing an important advantage over merely beginning with the premise that wrongdoers forfeit rights. First, in terms of Hohfeldian logic, acquiring a duty is equivalent to losing a liberty right. Beginning with the premise that wrongdoers acquire a (remedial) duty is therefore tantamount to assuming that wrongdoers forfeit a liberty right. Tadros's argument thus begins by assuming the forfeiture of a liberty right and then concludes with the forfeiture of a claim right against punishment. But critics who find forfeiture mysterious are unlikely to take much comfort in an argument that begins by presuming that wrongdoers forfeit liberty rights.

At this point, Tadros might respond that, while acquiring a duty may be logically equivalent to losing a liberty right, it is far more perspicuous to describe the initial change in the wrongdoer's moral status as an acquisition of duty than as a loss of a liberty. For the sake of argument, let us suppose that this is correct. Even so, why think the acquisition of duties is any less mysterious than the forfeiture of rights? Personally, I do not think there is anything curious or otherwise problematic about supposing that one can incur a secondary duty when one breaches one's primary duty; my point is only that a critic who *does* question whether wrongdoers forfeit rights is likely to be equally skeptical of the assertion that wrongdoers acquire duties. And finally, even if the acquisition of duties somehow invites less controversy than the forfeiture of rights, it is hard to see why the former would be so much less mysterious that it would be worth the additional exposure to criticism to which Tadros is vulnerable in virtue of his needing to supply an argument from the acquisition of a duty to the forfeiture of a right against punishment. (Remember: while I have presumed for the sake of argument that this portion of his argument is sound, a number of critics have been much less generous.)[20]

In light of this, I prefer to begin by simply (and openly) assuming that wrongdoers forfeit rights. As I make plain in the introduction, I take for granted that there are moral rights and that these rights can be waived, they can be forfeited, and they are vulnerable to being overridden. Reasonable people can certainly disagree about whether we can waive and/or forfeit all of our rights, but I do not take myself to be saying anything contentious when I posit that at least some rights can be waived and forfeited. Indeed, unlike esoteric moral concepts like the "suberogatory," ordinary folks who have never set foot in a philosophy class understand perfectly well what it means to say that "Jane waived her right against being punched when she agreed to the boxing match" or "Jennifer forfeited her right against punishment when she stole the victim's laptop." If there is something fundamentally mysterious about how forfeiture operates, it strikes me as no more mysterious than how waiving works, and virtually no one doubts that we routinely waive our rights. Thus, the building blocks of the theory of punishment I seek to defend are commonly used and universally understood moral concepts, rather than the labored contortions of an academic philosopher who is struggling to contrive some one-off solution to a specific problem. Even so, some might object that my approach is ad hoc or question-begging. After all, (1) not everyone will share my intuitions, and (2) some theories of rights appear to conflict with my premise.

As for those who deny that violating the rights of others alters the moral standing of the wrongdoers, we simply agree to disagree, and I must concede that my arguments will have no purchase with them. I am relatively sanguine about this possibility, though, because every argument in this area will require assumptions with which others may potentially disagree, and it strikes me that very few will actually deny this particular premise.[21] To establish this, it seems the best I can do is to offer a scenario and hope that readers will agree with my analysis. In view of this, imagine that Victim and Bystander are eating their lunches, when suddenly, without provocation, Wrongdoer punches Victim in the face and then runs off with Victim's briefcase. All that the rights forfeiture thesis alleges is that Wrongdoer's moral standing has changed in such a way that Victim (or perhaps the authorities) may now treat Wrongdoer in a manner that would have been impermissible before Wrongdoer struck Victim and stole her briefcase. That is, before Wrongdoer violated Victim's rights, Victim (or the authorities) could not permissibly do anything to Wrongdoer that she could not also do to Bystander, but this is no longer the case. Finally, the forfeiture theorist claims that the reason Victim (or the authorities) may now treat Wrongdoer in ways that she (or they) cannot treat Bystander is because, in acting the way she did, Wrongdoer forfeited her rights against this treatment. Admittedly, not everyone will agree with this analysis, but it strikes me as merely commonsensical. In any event, this analysis is my starting place, and those who find it counterintuitive will receive no arguments designed to change their minds on this foundational claim.

As for (2), most believe that right-holders qualify for their rights in virtue of having some status (e.g., in virtue of being human beings or having the capacity for rationality or autonomy), and rights forfeiture appears to fly in the face of this, because the wrongdoer does not seem any less of a human or to have lost her capacity for rationality/autonomy. So how could she have lost her rights? This problem is sometimes referred to as "the problem of status." But notice: forfeiture theory need not deny that we qualify for moral rights in virtue of our status as human beings or rational/autonomous agents; it conflicts only with the view that we qualify for *nonforfeitable* rights in virtue of that status. So the question is not whether we qualify for rights in virtue of our status; it is what *type* of right we qualify for as rational agents or human beings. And to settle this question, it seems the best one can do is simply to return to one's considered convictions; as the scenario involving Wrongdoer, Victim, and Bystander was designed to show, it seems obvious that rational/human beings qualify for rights that can be forfeited by wrongdoing. Given this, perhaps we should say that our *fundamental* moral status as a person or rational/autonomous being is what makes us the type of thing that qualifies for moral rights in general, but that the specific moral rights we currently enjoy is a function of our behavior. Thus, just as Bill Gates can alter his specific moral rights by waiving the right to his money (when he promises to fund my venture, for instance) without changing his fundamental moral status, Wrongdoer can change her specific moral rights by forfeiting her right not to be punished (when she steals Victim's briefcase) without changing her fundamental moral status. If so, culpable people may have fewer rights than nonculpable people even though both are rational/autonomous human beings.

Finally, my strategy of presuming rather than arguing for the claim that rights can be forfeited raises the following question: If the core premise of rights forfeiture is as obvious and self-evident as I allege, then why has the forfeiture theory of punishment attracted so few advocates? Any answer I proffer here will obviously be speculative, but I do have some thoughts. First, it is important to distinguish between the modest claim that moral rights can be forfeited (which I assume for the sake of argument) and the more ambitious contention that rights forfeiture theory provides the best answer to the question of why we may permissibly punish (for which I argue). Although I expect most to accept the former, it alone is not sufficient to establish the latter. I suspect that many legal theorists reject the rights forfeiture theory of punishment—despite believing that rights can be forfeited—because they are (wrongly, as I argue) impressed by at least one of the standard objections against the forfeiture theory of punishment.

Another reason that rights forfeiture theory has garnered so few advocates may stem from a historical accident: the major fault lines in the literature on the morality of punishment emerged in the 1960s, well before focusing on moral rights was *en vogue*. The two main ethical camps when punishment was being explored were utilitarianism and Kantian deontology, so it is not surprising that the two dominant accounts of punishment are deterrence and retributivism. Still, it is somewhat surprising that more theorists have not migrated to forfeiture theory in the past several decades as talk of rights has become ubiquitous, but perhaps that is merely because most scholars enter the punishment debate via the canonical literature.

THE PROBLEM OF INDETERMINATE AUTHORIZATION

The next worry about rights forfeiture theory is sometimes called the problem of indeterminate authorization: If a criminal forfeits her rights, then presumably *anyone*—not just the state—may permissibly punish her. As a consequence, this view opens the door to vigilantism. The idea behind this objection is that we must reject forfeiture theory—no matter how well it might answer the question "Why may we punish?"—because it generates an absurd response to the question "Who may punish?" Here my answer is simple: forfeiture theory is guilty as charged; it does not necessarily rule out vigilantism.[22] But why think that this is a problem?

A central and enduring question of political philosophy is whether and why the state enjoys a monopoly on the permissible use of punishment. (This question occupied the entire first part of Nozick's *Anarchy, State and Utopia,* for instance.) Thus, given that the permissibility of vigilantism is none other than the fundamental debate between anarchism and statism, it strikes me that we should be suspicious of any theory of punishment that *did* antecedently rule out anarchism. I will argue in the next chapter that we can build upon a rights forfeiture foundation to explain the impermissibility of vigilantism for citizens of a legitimate state. Crucially, though, these are not arguments to which all forfeiture theorists must be committed; they are distinct considerations of political philosophy. Perhaps we should not be surprised that philosophers of law (who have been the principal authors of the literature on punishment) would take statism for granted, since the anarchism/statism debate is a core issue of political, not legal, philosophy.[23]

Finally, to those who remain inclined to reject forfeiture theory because it does not in itself explain why only the state may punish, it is worth pointing out that other approaches are equally silent on this question. Take retributivism, for instance. While most retributivists are presumably statists, some are not. In other words, the question of anarchism versus statism is an intramural debate that retributivists can have among themselves, and no retributivist accuses another of failing to be a retributivist because of her stance on this question. More important for my purposes here, no one rejects retributivism as a theory of punishment merely because it is compatible with anarchism. On the contrary, to the extent that theorists attend to the question "Who may punish?" they recognize that retributivists must supply extraretributive (though perhaps retributivism-related) considerations to explain the necessity of statism. And if we all understand that retributivism's failure to rule out anarchism gives us no reason to reject retributivism, why not extend the same courtesy to forfeiture theory?

THE PROBLEM OF SUITABILITY

The next objection, the problem of suitability, accuses rights forfeiture theory of implausibly suggesting that it is permissible for authorities to kill killers, rape rapists, and torture torturers. After all, if wrongdoers forfeit those rights that they have violated, then this approach appears to provide no reason why the authorities should not impose upon grievous wrongdoers the same gruesome treatment they inflicted on their victims.

My response to this objection is threefold. First, I am no cheerleader for the death penalty, and I certainly would not advocate state officials raping rapists or torturing torturers, but I am not convinced that this is because killers, rapists, and torturers do not forfeit their rights against being killed, raped, and tortured. To be clear: I am not insisting that killers necessarily *do* forfeit their right to life; I am merely suggesting that it is hard to rule this out. In my view, this is the type of thing about which reasonable people can disagree (and it seems objectionable to say that one is necessarily unreasonable if one believes that these core rights can possibly be forfeited). Indeed, one common complaint about the international criminal legal system's movement toward prosecuting and punishing the political and military leaders responsible for the worst human rights atrocities is that *no* punishment could suffice, given the magnitude of the evils perpetrated by these moral monsters. I am an enthusiastic supporter of international criminal law, but I must confess that I have some sympathy for this familiar sentiment. Even if I did not, though, it is not clear how one could establish the unreasonableness of the claim that Hitler, for instance, forfeited his right not to be tortured to death. How can one rationally defeat the claim that the members of the paramilitary groups in the former Yugoslavia who engaged in mass rape as an element of their campaign of so-called ethnic cleansing forfeited their rights against being raped?

Again, in conceding the difficulty (if not the impossibility) of conclusively defeating these claims, I am not insisting that there are no limits on which rights these wrongdoers forfeited. Even if there were no such limits, however, it would not follow that forfeiture theorists would necessarily be committed to recommending these draconian punishments, because there are a variety of obvious practical, policy, and perhaps even principled reasons why we should not want our legal authorities killing killers, raping rapists, and torturing torturers.[24]

Finally, the most direct response to the problem of suitability is to emphasize that we need not construe forfeiture theory as the claim that the wrongdoer forfeits *precisely the same* right that she herself violates. This is admittedly one especially salient brand of rights forfeiture theory, and certainly some forfeiture theorists have championed this view, but it is clearly not the only option. I will say more about this in response to the next objection, but for now it suffices to note that, just as some but not all retributivists endorse the *lex talionis* principle, rights forfeiture theorists need not insist that the wrongdoer necessarily forfeits all and only those particular rights she violates.[25] To emphasize: forfeiture theorists are committed to the general claim that a wrongdoer forfeits some of her rights, but this general proposition must not be confused with the more specific claim (which some rights forfeiture theorists have admittedly endorsed) that a wrongdoer forfeits all and only those rights she herself has violated.[26] Given this, there is no reason why a forfeiture theorist must claim that a murderer forfeits her right against being killed or that a torturer has no right not to be tortured. It would admittedly be odd for rights forfeiture theorists to contend that a murderer or torturer has forfeited *none* of her rights (If you do not forfeit any rights when you murder or torture, when would you?), but forfeiture theorists can espouse various accounts of which particular rights the murderer and torturer forfeit.

THE PROBLEM OF DURATION AND BREADTH

The next objection, the problem of duration and breadth, poses a related but distinct problem for rights forfeiture theory. This concern is sometimes registered in terms of this theory's inability to provide plausible answers to the following two questions: Do criminals forfeit their rights temporarily or permanently? Do they forfeit their rights broadly or narrowly? To see why these questions are thought to be so problematic, imagine that Tom kidnaps Jerry for three days. Can Tom be imprisoned permanently or only temporarily? Permanent incarceration seems excessive, but the only nonarbitrary temporary jail sentence is three days, which seems woefully insufficient. Similarly, imagine that Itchy steals $5 from Scratchy. Has Itchy forfeited all or only a portion of her property rights? If we say all, that seems excessive, but if we say some, the only nonarbitrary punishment is a fine of $5, which is clearly insufficient.

Given my analysis of the previous objection, it should be clear that forfeiture theorists can easily sidestep this worry by simply denying that the criminal must be understood to have forfeited *that particular* right that she herself violated. Punishment of three days in prison for Tom and a $5 fine for Itchy may well be the most obvious or salient responses, but rights forfeiture theorists need not understand their theories in the simplest, most formulaic terms. It seems more plausible for a forfeiture theorist to insist merely that a wrongdoer forfeits her right against a *fitting* or *proportionate* punishment.

At this point a critic might understandably wonder what precisely is a "fitting" or a "proportionate" punishment for any given crime, and how do we go about discovering this. Other forfeiture theorists may have an easy answer to this question, but I do not. I would hasten to add, however, that while my lack of a ready answer to this particular query might be regarded as suspiciously convenient, it is not ad hoc. Nor is this issue specific to rights forfeiture theory. The most sophisticated retributivists routinely shy away from offering precise punishments for specific crimes, for instance, and as Daniel McDermott has noted, "the problem of matching crime with punishment has occupied philosophers for centuries, and any theory of punishment that offered a simple formula for determining punishments should be immediately suspect."[27] What is more, this lack of precision extends beyond the domain of punishment. Indeed, intuitionists from W. D. Ross to Russ Shafer-Landau have contended that, while general moral principles are self-evident, verdictive moral conclusions are not. So if this inability to supply obvious and self-evident conclusions at every level is prevalent not only within the literature on punishment but across the field of (meta)ethics more generally, my inability to supply a simple formula for determining which specific rights are forfeited by any given wrong is not ad hoc and should not be regarded as a distinctive weakness of the forfeiture theory of punishment. In sum, then, while my response to the problem of duration and breadth reveals that forfeiture theory may not be as simple and powerful as some might like it to be, the theory cannot be rejected for recommending that wrongdoers must be punished either too leniently or too harshly.

THE PROBLEM OF RIGHTS TYPE

The last objection I want to consider, the problem of rights type, has been raised by David Boonin in *The Problem of Punishment*.[28] Boonin asks whether a wrongdoer forfeits a *legal* right by violating a *legal* right or forfeits a *moral* right by violating a *moral* right. Unfortunately for the rights forfeiture theorist, neither answer appears plausible. We cannot be speaking only of legal rights, because we want to know why it is *morally*, not just legally, permissible to punish. But if it is morally permissible to punish people as long as they violate a moral right, then forfeiture theory apparently recommends state punishment in at least three types of awkward case: (1) when someone is morally guilty but legally innocent; (2) when someone violates a relatively inconsequential moral right, as when I steal a potato chip off of a friend's plate at lunch; and (3) when someone commits a paradigmatically "private" wrong, as when a spouse commits adultery. Let us consider each of these cases in turn.

Permitting the state to punish someone who is legally innocent is problematic only if we have a right not to be punished unless we break the law, but is there such a right? At first blush, it certainly seems so. After all, the unfairness of punishing someone for conduct that is either not illegal or not easily known to be illegal explains our insistence that criminal law be clear, promulgated, and prospectively applied. Imagine if we criminally punished Nancy for failing to come to a complete stop at a deserted intersection if there were no stop sign, stop light, or any other legal requirement (or even presumption) that one stop at all intersections. It seems safe to conclude, then, that one has a right not to be punished unless one breaks the law, and thus it would be problematic if forfeiture theory permitted one to be punished as long as one had merely violated a moral right.

This conclusion may be too quick, though. From the practical and policy perspectives, it would certainly be preferable to punish only lawbreakers, but because not all offenses are like Nancy's failure to stop at a deserted intersection, there may be some cases for which there is no principled objection to punishing the legally innocent. Think of the defendants at Nuremberg, for instance. Because (some of) their conduct was contrary to neither existing German nor international criminal law, some of these Nazi officials were legally innocent. Did they therefore have a right not to be punished? It is not so clear. While we may have qualms about punishing Nancy for failing to stop at the deserted intersection because it seems unfair to assume that she should have known to do so in the absence of a clear law requiring that one stop in those circumstances, it does not seem similarly unfair to expect those who commit unspeakable atrocities to know that they are behaving culpably, and thus are rendering themselves liable to punishment. David Luban has recently argued along these lines. As he puts it, "my basic response to the fair-notice argument is that when the deed is morally outrageous—*malum in se*, as criminal lawyers say—then no reasonable expectations of the defendants are violated when they are tried for it."[29] With respect to Nuremberg in particular, Luban concludes that "though there is no getting around the fact that the Nuremberg Tribunal applied law retroactively, it did not treat the defendants worse than they had reason to expect, which is the moral basis for the ban on retroactivity."[30]

I am inclined to agree with Luban on this point: Whether or not one may permissibly be punished for actions that were not at the time illegal seems to me to depend on the nature of one's conduct. If one commits a sufficiently despicable act, then perhaps one has no right not to be punished. For the sake of argument, however, let us assume that Luban is wrong about this. That is, let us grant that no matter what wrong one commits, fairness (or perhaps some other consideration) explains why one retains the right not to be punished unless one also breaks the law. If this were the case, would it be problematic for rights forfeiture theory? Not at all. If there is some story we can tell to explain why legal guilt is always necessary for punishment to be justified, then forfeiture theorists can simply invoke this story to explain why those who are legally innocent retain their rights not to be punished. To recapitulate: As Luban's analysis of the defendants at Nuremberg illustrates, Boonin may be too quick to assume that it is always impermissible to punish those who are legally innocent. And even if Boonin is correct that those who have not broken the law may never be punished, it is unclear why forfeiture theorists cannot help themselves to whatever reasons support this fact to establish why they, too, would insist that the legally innocent have not forfeited their right not to be punished.

Boonin's second concern about asserting that one forfeits one's moral right not to be punished as long as one violates a victim's moral rights is that it would license the state to punish defendants for having violated even utterly trivial rights. Imagine, for instance, that I steal a potato chip off of Zach's plate while we are at lunch together. Assuming that Zach did not give me permission to take his potato chip, I violated his right in helping myself to it. The forfeiture theorist appears unable to explain why the state may not punish me for this transgression. But this seems absurd. Virtually everyone who works in this area affirms de minimis, the doctrine that one should not be legally punished for trivial offenses.

I concede both that states should not be in the business of punishing trivial offenses and that rights forfeiture theory appears unable to explain why this is so. It is not clear, however, that any theory of punishment fares better on this score. As Doug Husak has recently argued, it is extremely difficult to find any principled reason that de minimis crimes may not permissibly be punished.[31] If states should not be in the business of criminally prosecuting and punishing defendants for trivial crimes, this is only because the criminal law is such a blunt instrument that it could not help but severely overpunish someone for an offense as minor as stealing a potato chip. To emphasize: given the limited utensils a prosecuting attorney has at her disposal, there is no punishment she could recommend that would not be grossly disproportionate to such a minor transgression. Because of this, and given that it would be a horribly inefficient utilization of funds if our criminal system were to concern itself with such trivial matters, we have compelling *practical* (but no purely principled) reasons to insist that states refrain from criminally prosecuting de minimis offenses.

It is also worth noting that our concerns about the state punishing defendants for trivial crimes do not necessarily apply to nonstate actors, so it remains an open question as to whether others (perhaps Zach, for instance) might permissibly punish me for stealing a potato chip. This is a possibility from which I do not shrink. In my view, tiny rights violations may well lead to correspondingly small forfeitures, and thus there seems nothing awkward about supposing that Zach would perhaps be entitled to unilaterally help himself to a bit of food off of my plate only because I forfeited my moral dominion over my lunch when I stole some of his. This is not a position to which I am necessarily committed; I mention it only because it is consistent with rights forfeiture theory and, unlike the idea of *state* punishment for such a minor offense, it seems fairly plausible.

Boonin's third worry about suggesting that one is morally liable to punishment as long as one violates a moral right is that it opens the door to the permissibility of the state's punishing defendants for committing so-called private wrongs, such as lying or breaking a promise. Imagine, for instance, that Jennifer commits adultery after promising her husband, Jake, that she will be faithful to him. Given Jennifer's pledge, her extramarital sex violated Jake's right that she remain monogamous. But it seems awkward to claim that the state may permissibly punish Jennifer in this case. No matter how culpable she may be for cheating on Jake, it is simply not the state's business to pass judgment, let alone to punish Jennifer for her infidelity.

I explore this issue at greater length in chapter 4. For now, let me simply register my doubts that any wrongs are distinctively private. For the sake of argument, however, let us assume that marital infidelities and other qualifying broken promises are in fact purely private matters. Why think that this truth poses a problem for rights forfeiture theory? If there is a good argument that explains why states should not punish cheating spouses, then why assume that forfeiture theorists cannot simply invoke that argument to explain why their view does not commit them to punishing rights violators in this case? Or if others are free to simply assume without argument that states have principled reasons to refrain from punishing "private" rights violations, why can a forfeiture theorist not also help herself to this assumption? To emphasize: In the absence of some explanation as to why this argument for (or assumption of) the morally significant distinction between public and private wrongs is inaccessible to a forfeiture theorist, this distinction gives us no reason to question the truth of rights forfeiture theory.

Indeed, if anything, it seems to me that forfeiture theory is particularly *well* positioned to counter this potential criticism. To appreciate this, recall that rights forfeiture theory is not a justification for *state* punishment; it is merely a justification for punishment. As explained above, it is an open question whether forfeiture theorists should endorse statism or anarchism. Given this, it is unwarranted to infer from forfeiture theory's conclusion that I may permissibly be punished for stealing a potato chip or cheating on my partner that forfeiture theory is committed to the *state* punishing me for these trivial and/or "private" rights violations. What is more, it is especially interesting to see critics like Boonin raise these concerns so shortly after protesting that forfeiture theory must be dismissed for its compatibility with vigilantism. After all, how can Boonin criticize rights forfeiture theory for its inability to rule out nonstate agents' meting out the punishments and simultaneously object that this approach must be abandoned because it implies that states should necessarily do all of the punishing? I have argued that forfeiture theory is vulnerable to neither attack, but clearly it cannot be dismissed on both grounds at the same time.

WHITHER THE THEORY?

Even if a reader is satisfied with all of my analysis so far, a new question emerges: Does the rights forfeiture thesis really provide a theory of punishment? In responding to these standard objections, time and again I have insisted that it is not the business of rights forfeiture theory to supply an answer. Against the worry about anarchism, I have suggested that forfeiture theory can remain agnostic on the anarchism versus statism debate; in response to concerns about unsuitable, lenient, or excessive punishments, I have insisted that forfeiture theory itself need take no stand on which particular rights are forfeited; in the face of worries about the state punishing private wrongs, I have been noncommittal on the public/private distinction; and so on. Even if each of these individual responses is fair, a critic might worry about their cumulative result. Put bluntly, it now appears that rights forfeiture does so little—it answers so few of our questions—that it hardly qualifies as a *theory* of punishment. After all, how can I claim to be defending a theory of punishment if rights forfeiture tells us so little about who, when, and how much we may punish?

This is a legitimate question, but there are several things that can be said in response. First, to the extent that I am inclined to agree that the forfeiture approach does not constitute a theory of punishment, it is only because I am tempted to regard it as a *family* of theories. Indeed, retributivism strikes me as more of a group of theories than a single theory, so perhaps we should say the same about rights forfeiture accounts. Second and perhaps most important, this comparison reminds us that there seems to be something of a double standard at play here. Everyone appreciates that there is plenty of room for intramural disagreement among retributivists, restitutivists, and consequentialists, but critics of rights forfeiture seem to presume that forfeiture theory must take one particular (and often particularly implausible) form. If any given retributivist recommends anarchism, for instance, then critics may well attack *that particular version* of retributivism, but they do not (mis)understand themselves to be rejecting retributivism as a whole. Unfortunately, the same cannot be said for opponents of rights forfeiture theory, who all too often fasten upon one distinctive version of forfeiture theory that they regard as absurd and then conclude that they have thereby defeated forfeiture theory as a whole. What explains this double standard? Perhaps it has arisen because, with so few defenders of rights forfeiture theory, commentators do not recognize that it is a family of views within which there is plenty of room for vigorous debate among family members. In any event, I would urge that we turn this last potential objection on its head: rather than insist that rights forfeiture cannot qualify as a theory of punishment because it leaves open many important questions about punishment, we should appreciate that forfeiture is a family of theories, whose virtues and liabilities should be assessed in the same way that we evaluate the more traditional approaches to the morality of punishment.

Finally, while one can endorse the general thesis that rights forfeiture is necessary and sufficient (or merely necessary, if one endorses only a weak version of forfeiture theory) to explain the permissibility of punishment without taking a stand on many of these controversial issues, presumably most of these questions will be answered by the specific account one defends. As I will argue in the remaining chapters, for instance, the particular theory I favor (1) is statist, (2) is limited-reasons, (3) does not require one to have violated someone else's right, (4) regards the executive right in the state of nature to be competitive, and (5) eschews the rights forfeiture analogue of the *lex talionis* principle in favor of a less formulaic specification of which particular rights are forfeited by any given wrongful act. And this more specific version of forfeiture theory provides definitive answers to virtually all of the questions raised by the various standard objections. Some of these answers will of course be controversial (even among fellow forfeiture theorists), but my principal goal to this point has not been to defend this particular version of rights forfeiture. More minimally, I have sought to vindicate forfeiture theory in general, and I shall thus be gratified if readers are merely more receptive to the idea that we should focus less on the desirable aims that punishment might achieve and more on the rights that morally constrain any permissible system of criminal law.

Chapter 3

State Punishment and International Criminal Law

Chapter 2 defended the rights forfeiture theory of punishment. But even if we agree that punishment is permissible just in case the person punished has forfeited her right against this hard treatment, it remains an open question *who* may mete out the punishment. As chapter 2's discussion of vigilantism highlights, it does not follow from the fact that punishment is permissible that the *state* should be doing the punishing. Imagine, for instance, that Anna assaults Betty. It seems correct that Betty may now treat Anna in ways that would have been impermissible before the assault, but it does not follow that some random third party, say, Claire, may permissibly punish Anna. And if Claire may not punish Anna, what gives the state the right to insert itself into a private matter between Anna and Betty? The point here is that, although Anna may not righteously object if Betty punishes her, perhaps Anna retains her dominion over third parties. What is more, even if Anna cannot object to third parties meting out the punishment, perhaps Betty has a right to complain. If anyone occupies an advantaged position over Anna, presumably it is Betty. Perhaps Betty has an *exclusive* right to punish Anna and, unless Betty freely delegates her authority to someone else, no third party may unilaterally take it upon herself to punish Anna. In brief, even if forfeiture theory explains the permissibility of *the victim's* imposing the hard treatment of punishment, it does not necessarily justify the state's (or any other third party's) doling out the punishment. We thus face a second rights question: Why does state punishment not violate the rights of the victim?

One standard response to this objection is to assert that the state may permissibly punish a criminal because *any* third party is permitted to do so. In terms of the example just offered, this line of argument suggests that it is not so difficult to explain why the state may punish Anna, because everyone (not just Betty) has the right to punish Anna for assaulting Betty. Thus, in response to the question "What gives the state the right to punish Anna when Claire may not?" the appropriate response is thought to be "Nothing sets the state apart from Claire, but this is no problem because Claire also has the right to punish Anna."

The adequacy of this response obviously depends upon whether everyone or only direct victims have the right to punish wrongdoers in the state of nature, and this, in my view, is something about which reasonable people can disagree. Some believe that the victim occupies a unique, privileged position over anyone who has violated her rights, and that this special standing is best captured in terms of having an exclusive right to punish. There are times when Locke seems to suggest that only the victim has an executive right, but most of what he writes is more in keeping with the idea that anyone may punish criminals. (In the contemporary literature, Murray Rothbard adopts the former route, but Nozick and Simmons endorse the latter.)[1] I am inclined to agree with the Nozick/Simmons position that, while the victim has a special standing, this privileged position should not be cashed out in terms of an exclusive right to punish. The first thing to say in defense of this view is that there are various ways to recognize a victim's special status. If one distinguishes between a right to punish and a right to reparation, for instance, one can suggest that the victim's elevated standing should be understood wholly in terms of the latter. That is, one might conclude that, although anyone may punish the criminal, only the victim is entitled to reparation from him. What is more, conceiving of a victim's special standing solely in terms of reparation enables one to avoid a number of unpalatable implications. Specifically, if only the victim may permissibly punish a criminal, it seems to follow that a criminal could preserve his moral immunity against punishment by simply killing all of his victims. What is more, if the victim has an exclusive executive right, then her decision to pardon a criminal for his transgressions would make it impermissible for anyone to punish him. Perhaps neither of these conclusions is absurd, but both seem awkward.

Thus, both because cashing out a victim's special standing in terms of reparation enables us to capture the intuition that victims occupy a distinctive privileged position vis-à-vis those who have violated their rights, and because explaining a victim's elevated status in terms of an exclusive executive right has awkward implications, I am inclined toward the view that everyone in the state of nature has an executive right. And if anyone may punish wrongdoers, we do not need a fancy story to explain why the state violates neither the criminal's nor the victim's rights when it assigns itself the task of punishing wrongdoers. Put in terms of our example above, the state is just like Claire (or any other third party, for that matter) in having the right to punish Anna for violating Betty's rights.

Even if we assume that the best understanding of the natural executive right includes the idea that everyone (and not merely the victim) has the right to punish wrongdoers, this in itself is not enough to justify state punishment. More specifically, while this move might well justify the *state's punishing*, it does not justify the entire institution of *state punishment*. The problem, of course, is that positing a general executive right implies only what Simmons calls a "competitive" right to punish: everyone has the authority to punish wrongdoers, but no one may rightfully demand that others let her do the punishing. The basic idea here is that whoever gets to the wrongdoer first may permissibly punish her, and she violates no one else's right (i.e., she does not violate the victim's exclusive right to punish) when she does so. The problem that remains, however, is that states do not merely claim a *competitive* right to punish; they claim an *exclusive* right. States not only assert the authority to punish if they happen to be the first on the scene, they insist that anyone who arrives before them must refrain from punishing so that the state can do so. Indeed, states claim much more even than this. Not only do they claim the right to be the sole party authorized to mete out the appropriate punishment, they also claim the exclusive right to determine what the appropriate punishment is.

In fact, states understand their dominion in this arena to be so extensive that they claim the right to pardon wrongdoers. In other words, states assert that even if a given wrongdoer has no right not to be punished (indeed, even if this criminal is found *by the state* to have no claim against punishment), all others (including the victim) have a duty not to punish this criminal if the state pardons her. Finally, in order to have the power required to enforce this incredibly extensive, exclusive executive right, the state claims the right to help itself to a share of all of its constituents' assets, so that it has enough money to employ the armies of people necessary to ensure that everyone respects its sovereignty over this domain. To recapitulate: even if we conceive of the natural executive right as a general right enjoyed by everyone, this appears at most to give states a competitive liberty to punish criminals; it does not justify anything like the institution of state punishment.

It should now be apparent that those who seek to justify state punishment face the following dilemma. The natural executive right can be understood either as a special, exclusive right or as a general, competitive right. Because of the extensive dominion that states claim for themselves, defenders of state punishment might initially be tempted to understand the natural executive right in the first manner. But if the right to punish is a special, exclusive right, presumably it is held by the *victim* rather than some third party, and thus it is unclear how the state could ever permissibly punish a criminal. If we understand the natural right to punish as a general right held by everyone, on the other hand, we can explain the state's permissibly punishing criminals. But then the state has only a competitive right to punish, which is dramatically less than the unrivalled sovereignty it claims. Either way, we appear unable to justify anything like the institution of state punishment.

It is important to appreciate, however, that this dilemma does not prove that state punishment cannot be justified; more minimally, it shows only that anyone who seeks to defend the institution of state punishment owes us a story of how the state comes to acquire an exclusive, executive right that initially resides either exclusively with the victim or (more plausibly, I think) generally with each of us. The traditional Lockean response is that this transfer takes place only in the case of some voluntary transaction, such as a morally valid social contract. This type of account will not suffice, however, because, as most now acknowledge, there has not in fact been any such voluntary transaction between existing states and their constituents. And once one concedes this, there appear to be only two salient options. You can either stick to your Lockean guns (as John Simmons does, for instance) and insist that no existing state has an exclusive right to punish wrongdoers, or you can offer some nonvoluntarist account of the state's exclusive, executive right. Because I would like to avoid the anarchism on which Simmons ultimately settles, I will try to explain how a state can acquire the exclusive right to punish.

My own view is that one can justify the state's exclusive dominion over the punitive process only if one takes stock of the aims of punishment, the importance of these aims, and a state's unparalleled ability to accomplish these aims without imposing unreasonable burdens upon its constituents. In light of this, let us begin by clarifying why we want to punish criminals. It strikes me that each of the standard theories of punishment supplies a different part of a plausible answer to this question. That is, we are interested in punishing criminals because doing so (1) deters everyone from committing crimes, (2) serves justice by giving criminals the hard treatment they deserve, (3) helps to morally educate both the criminal and society at large, (4) allows society to express its moral values, (5) helps restore the victims along with their friends and families, and, finally, (6) provides an effective, peaceful outlet for what would otherwise be socially disruptive tensions. Although each of the traditional theories helps illuminate what we stand to gain from an effective institution of punishment, I think that deterrence is by far the most significant.[2] Indeed, I believe that it alone is necessary and sufficient. Putting this point in terms of human rights, I contend both that (1) if the state's exclusive control over punishment were necessary to secure everyone's human rights, then it could be justified *even if it did not do a particularly good job of realizing the other five aims outlined above,* and that (2) if state sovereignty was either not necessary or not sufficient to secure everyone's human rights, then it could not be justified even if it was necessary and sufficient to adequately realize the other five aims. Still, these other aims are not irrelevant, because they are desirable goods, and thus it may buttress the case for state control over punishment if such dominion helps us realize these additional goods.

With this understanding of the aims of punishment, we are now in a better position to see why we might favor a state monopoly in this arena. If the state is justified in inserting itself, it must be because these six aims—particularly deterrence—can be more fully realized with a system of state punishment than if individuals were left to their own devices. The crucial point is that (as social contract theorists have historically emphasized) things would deteriorate into a horribly dangerous mess if each individual were personally responsible for punishing those who wronged him. In particular, crime would likely increase dramatically as would-be criminals capitalized on the greater chances of escaping detection and punishment. Plus, victims who personally mete out the punishment are more likely to punish the innocent and overpunish the guilty. Not only are justice and deterrence better served, it seems clear that aims such as moral education, a societal safety valve, and societal expression of values could scarcely be achieved at all in the absence of a state monopoly on punishment. In short, all six aims stand to be adequately realized only in a system with an authoritative body that makes, enforces, and impartially adjudicates promulgated rules.[3]

If governmental control over the institution of punishment will allow us better to achieve our six aims of punishment, we have a case for the state's nonconsensually taking exclusive control over the punitive process. As it stands, however, this case is insufficient. The state's ability to best realize the aims of a process does not automatically give it the right to interfere in people's affairs. The fact that others could do a decidedly better job of tending my garden or decorating my house does not give them the right to push me aside and take over these projects, for example. Our commitment to my rights in these instances is indicative of our general regard for personal sovereignty; we recognize that each person's moral dominion over her own life gives her the right to manage her affairs even when others might do so better. Thus, we need a special explanation for why the state may nonconsensually co-opt the punishment process from various individuals merely because it is better equipped to manage the task. In the absence of such an account, Betty appears just as entitled to (less than optimally) punish Anna as she is to (less than optimally) tend her garden and decorate her house.

The special ingredient in the recipe for political legitimacy involves the profound importance of the aims involved: there is a crucial difference between the consequences of my managing my home and garden and the consequences of my imposing my own punishments upon those who (I believe) violate my rights. While there might be others who would do a better job of completing the tasks involved in each portion of my life, the realm of punishment is distinguished by the high stakes involved not only for me, but for those around me. If each of us does a less-than-optimal job in most areas of our lives, no great collective harm is done. If we all individually did our suboptimal jobs punishing others, on the other hand, the cumulative consequences would be quite grave. To transpose this standard lesson of social contract theory into the parlance of today: people would be imperiled in an environment in which their human rights were unprotected. It is the *gravity* of this particular issue, then, that distinguishes punishment from other matters and helps explain why the individual moral dominion that typically prevails against the expertise of third parties is insufficient in this realm. More precisely, it is not merely the gravity of the consequences, it is also the fact that these consequences are not solely personal. In other words, it is crucial that *others* are imperiled in the absence of a state that satisfactorily secures the gravely important aims of a system of punishment.[4]

In the end, then, the reason that a state violates no rights when it nonconsensually inserts itself into what might appear to be a private matter between Anna and Betty is because of the three facts that (1) unlike Claire, the state is uniquely qualified maximally to realize the aims of punishment; (2) unlike most matters of personal sovereignty, the aims of punishment are sufficiently important to others to outweigh the premium we rightly place on individual moral dominion; and (3) the state can satisfactorily realize these crucial aims without imposing unreasonable costs upon its constituents.

It is important to recognize that, even if this account adequately explains why *some* states enjoy an exclusive right to punish criminals, it by no means follows that *all* states have this right simply in virtue of being de facto states. An adequate defense of statism must be able to distinguish legitimate from illegitimate states, and presumably only the former would enjoy a moral right to preside over punishment. Because my account alleges that states are entitled to a monopoly in this arena in virtue of their unique ability to realize the important aims of punishment, it follows that a state has this right only if it is in fact able and willing adequately to realize these aims. Thus, because failed states are unable and rogue states are unwilling to manage the institution of punishment in a fashion that satisfactorily secures everyone's human rights, neither of these types of illegitimate states would qualify for the right in question.[5]

Finally, it is worth making explicit which rights citizens have and which they lack. In my view, constituents of legitimate states lack at least three important rights: (1) the right personally to punish wrongdoers, (2) the right to ensure that those who have wronged them are punished, and (3) the right that others not commandeer their money to help fund punishments. It should by now be clear that, unlike victims in the state of nature, the citizens of a legitimate state may not take punishment into their own hands. A less obvious implication of this conclusion, however, is that citizens have no right that their state punish the criminals who violated their rights. Consider again the scenario in which Anna violates Betty's rights. If this occurs in the state of nature, Betty may punish Anna or even get a third party to do so, as long as no one else has already punished her. Within the context of a legitimate state, though, Betty has no right to punish Anna even if the state elects *not* to do so (e.g., if the state decides not to charge Anna with the crime, fails to convict her, or even finds her guilty but subsequently pardons her). Thus, Betty not only lacks the right to be Anna's punisher, as a citizen in a legitimate state, Betty has no right that Anna be punished at all. Third and finally, while in the state of nature each of us has a right against others taking a portion of her assets in order to finance punishing wrongdoers (even if Claire needed the funds to track down and punish Anna for violating Betty's rights, for instance, Claire would simply be stealing if she took some of Betty's money without Betty's permission), citizens have no right to complain when their legitimate state helps itself to those funds needed to support its institution of punishment. In short, Betty's citizenship in a legitimate state entails that she has no right against taxation.[6]

Even if the state's moral authority is as extensive as outlined above, it is emphatically not unrestricted. In particular, while states may have the discretion not to punish guilty people, they are not similarly entitled to punish innocent persons. In other words, while citizens in legitimate states may have much less personal discretion over punishment, they retain the right not to be wrongly punished. To put this point in perspective, imagine that a legitimate state nonculpably but nonetheless mistakenly convicts Donna of the crime Anna in fact committed against Betty. Suppose that Donna later has the opportunity to escape from prison. In my view, Donna may permissibly seize this opportunity; she has no duty to accept the terms of the conviction, even if it was handed down by a legitimate state that in good faith found her to be guilty. If this is right, then Socrates may be correct that we are duty-bound to comply with the *just* laws of a legitimate state, but he was wrong to conclude that citizens have no right but to accept a wrongful punishment.

A POTENTIAL OBJECTION

A careful reader who is familiar with the literature on the morality of punishment may have noticed two important respects in which my account resembles H. L. A. Hart's theory, as articulated in "Prolegomenon to the Principles of Punishment." First, just as Hart distinguished the macro question "What justifies the general practice of punishment?" from the micro questions concerning "How should punishment be distributed?" I have distinguished the institutional question "Why does state punishment not violate the rights of others who might want to mete out the punishment themselves?" from the interactional question "Why does punishment not violate the rights of the person punished?" And just as Hart invoked the consequentialist theory of utilitarianism to answer his first question and the deontologically based retributivism to answer his second, I allege that the deontologically based right in the first case is outweighed by consequential considerations but the deontologically based right prevails in the second.

But notice: Casting my theory in these terms raises a potential concern about the role I claim consequential considerations play in overriding rights. Because I acknowledge that deontologically based rights can be defeated by sufficiently weighty consequential considerations, one might worry that my account suffers from the same sort of dialectical instability as Hart's. In Hart's case, the instability arises from his reliance on utilitarianism as a general justifying aim of punishment despite the clear inadequacy of its implications regarding the distribution of punishment. Does utilitarianism's unpalatable conclusions regarding the permissibility of punishing the innocent not reveal a fundamental flaw? If so, presumably this disqualifies utilitarianism as a viable candidate to answer *any* question about the morality of punishment. And if one insists that utilitarianism has not been disqualified, why may we not rely on it to answer questions about the distribution of punishment despite its counterintuitive implications? In my case, the worry might be expressed as follows: If the consequences I invoke are sufficient to explain why a victim's (deontologically based) rights are not violated when the state inserts itself into the punitive process, why cannot these same consequences equally explain why an innocent person's rights are not violated when she is wrongly punished? Put bluntly, if it is objectionable for Hart to favor consequences in one instance while relying on deontology in another, why I am entitled to do so?

My response to this challenge is twofold. First, it is important to recognize that Hart did not merely appeal to consequences; he relied more specifically on utilitarianism. This is important because, while I have indeed invoked the beneficial consequences of state punishment, I have never relied upon utilitarianism. More minimally, my theory depends upon what might be called "samaritanism."[7] My account is samaritan because, just as I might justify my commandeering your boat for twenty minutes if this were necessary to rescue a drowning swimmer, I have justified the state's monopolizing the punitive process only because this is necessary to rescue all of its constituents from an environment in which their human rights would be vulnerable. And while samaritanism is a *type* of consequential principle, it is considerably more restricted (and therefore less vulnerable to awkward counterexamples) than utilitarianism.

Second, notice that I do not utilize samaritanism at one stage of my argument only to reject it at another. Rather, I submit that samaritanism is always defensible, but it is *applicable* only in certain contexts. The reason I invoke it in my answer to only one of the two rights questions is thus simply because it is applicable in this context but not the other. To appreciate this point, notice that samaritanism would almost never justify criminally prosecuting and punishing an innocent person, because the hard treatment of punishment is so onerous that punishing an innocent person would impose an unreasonable burden upon that individual.[8] And since an imposition qualifies as samaritan only if it both (1) is necessary to rescue someone who is sufficiently imperiled, and (2) does not impose unreasonable costs on those whose normal spheres of dominion are curtailed in order to make the rescue possible, one cannot appeal to samaritanism to justify punishing the innocent.

In sum, while the combination of the rights forfeiture theory laid out in the previous chapter and my justification for statism, offered in this chapter, admittedly resembles Hart's hybrid position, it invokes samaritanism rather than utilitarianism. And although samaritanism is not applicable to both of the rights questions on which I focus here, at no point do I claim or imply that samaritanism generates unacceptable implications in any context where it does apply. Thus, despite the important similarities between Hart's and my accounts, my view cannot rightly be accused of suffering from the dialectical instability that undermines his theory.

INTERNATIONAL CRIMINAL LAW

If my account of state punishment explains why the constituents of a legitimate state must refrain from vigilantism, it presumably has analogous implications for various parties outside of the state. If so, the defense of statism outlined above has implications for international criminal law.[9] With this in mind, I would now like to explain how my rights account of state punishment confirms the inadequacy of the conventional understanding of international criminal law.

According to the prevailing view, external parties may not prosecute and punish a criminal unless her crime has some sort of border-crossing element. As Mary Robinson, the former United Nations high commissioner for human rights, puts it: "The principle of universal jurisdiction is based on the notion that certain crimes are so harmful to international interests that states are entitled—and even obliged—to bring proceedings against the perpetrator, regardless of the location of the crime or the nationality of the perpetrator or the victim."[10]

To see the error of this way of thinking, consider the rationale behind a paradigmatic international criminal offense, crimes against humanity. As Robinson's quote indicates, the category of crimes against humanity is regarded as necessary to explain an international party's jurisdiction over what would otherwise be the exclusive business of a sovereign state. This is because international lawyers typically approach these matters from a Westphalian perspective; they presume that each state enjoys a privileged position of moral dominion over its self-regarding affairs. And if each state is sovereign over its own matters, presumably external parties have a duty to respect a state's exercise of criminal law. In other words, it is up to each state to decide whether and how to prosecute its own criminals, even those responsible for human rights atrocities. To overcome this presumption in favor of state sovereignty, the international community must explain why certain forms of criminal activity do not merely affect members of a given state but also harm humanity as a whole. As its name implies, the category of crimes against humanity is thought to fulfill this function because it is said to pick out those crimes that (even if perpetrated exclusively by and against members of a single country) harm all of humanity. Geoffrey Robertson puts this point particularly clearly when he explains that the category of crimes against humanity provides "the key to unlock the closed door of state sovereignty, and to hold political leaders responsible for the great evils they visit upon humankind."[11]

Accounts of what constitutes a crime against humanity vary quite widely, of course, but in my estimation they all fail because none shows that humanity is actually harmed (in the morally relevant sense) by such a crime, no matter how horribly it violates its victims' rights.[12] Even if we concede that the genocide of Jews violates the humanity of those Jews attacked, or that using chemical weapons against Kurds shocks the conscience of humankind, for instance, neither conclusion is sufficient because neither account shows why an average citizen in Japan, say, is necessarily harmed by even the most horrific crime perpetrated against either a Jew in

Germany or a Kurd in Iraq. The basic problem is that, just as traditional philosophers of law have had a notoriously difficult time explaining how certain acts qualify as crimes (rather than mere torts) because they harm the entire political community, international lawyers seem unable to furnish a plausible explanation of how humanity is harmed in the morally relevant sense by putative "crimes against humanity."

Assuming that my concerns about the category of crimes against humanity are well-founded, does this show that we cannot justify the international prosecution and punishment of crimes that have no border-crossing elements? Not at all. Even if no account of crimes against humanity can explain why the international community has an actionable interest in the internal affairs of a state's criminal legal system, it does not necessarily follow that international criminal law is therefore unjustified. This is because the category of crimes against humanity is important only if one accepts the Westphalian assumption that all de facto states are entitled to dominion over their self-regarding affairs. But as the preceding analysis of state punishment illustrates, not all states enjoy a morally privileged position over their internal affairs; only *legitimate* states do. And if the Westphalian outlook is mistaken, the failure of accounts of crimes against humanity gives us no reason to doubt the permissibility of international criminal law. To emphasize: Unless one begins with the presumption that all de facto states have a moral right to sovereignty over their self-regarding affairs, one does not need a special category of crimes that purportedly harm all of humanity.

To appreciate this point, it is worth recalling why illegitimate states have no right to self-determination. As argued above, states are legitimate only if they satisfactorily protect the human rights of their constituents. If a state adequately performs these functions, then it enjoys a morally privileged position of dominion over its self-regarding affairs, including its system of criminal law. But if a state is either unable or unwilling to protect its constituents' human rights, then it is illegitimate and has no claim to sovereignty. Thus, neither Milosevic's Yugoslavia nor contemporary Somalia would qualify as legitimate because the former was unwilling and the latter is unable to protect the basic rights of its citizens. As a result, it would be permissible to forcibly impose international criminal law on either of these states. Most important for my purposes here, we would not have to demonstrate that criminals in Yugoslavia or Somalia were harming anyone outside of either state in order to justify this intervention. Instead, because neither of these states is legitimate, neither has a presumptive claim to self-determination that must be defeated by an account of how (some subset of) the crimes committed within these countries putatively harm all of humanity.

The bottom line is that when widespread or systematic rights violations are going unpunished within a given state, this state is not satisfactorily realizing the crucial aims of a criminal legal system. As a consequence, it has no claim to exclusive dominion over the punitive processes within its territory and thus cannot rightfully object if some external party takes it upon itself to prosecute and punish those who have violated the rights of others. My theory of state punishment thus has the following implication for international criminal law: Any state that satisfactorily realizes the vital aims of criminal punishment has a right to sovereignty in this realm that explains why no external party may unilaterally assign itself the task of prosecuting and punishing criminals within this state's territory. If widespread or systematic violations of rights are going unpunished in a particular state, on the other hand, then this state is not performing its requisite political functions, it is illegitimate, and it has no right that others not interfere with its system of criminal law.

If the theory of state punishment developed here is correct, this alternative understanding of criminal law enjoys a stronger theoretical foundation than the Westphalian orientation on which the prevailing conception has been built. What is more, this alternative account leaves no less room for the imposition of international criminal law. To see why, notice that article 7(1) of the Rome Statute of the International Criminal Court defines a crime against humanity as

> any of the following acts when committed as part of a widespread or systematic attack directed against any civilian population, with knowledge of the attack:
>
> (a) Murder;
> (b) Extermination;
> (c) Enslavement;
> (d) Deportation or forcible transfer of population;
> (e) Imprisonment or other severe deprivation of physical liberty in violation of fundamental rules of international law;
> (f) Torture;
> (g) Rape, sexual slavery, enforced prostitution, forced pregnancy, enforced sterilization, or any other form of sexual violence of comparable gravity;
> (h) Persecution against any identifiable group or collectivity on political, racial, national, ethnic, cultural, religious, gender as defined in paragraph 3, or other grounds that are universally recognized as impermissible under international law, in connection with any act referred to in this paragraph or any crime within the jurisdiction of the Court;
> (i) Enforced disappearance of persons;
> (j) The crime of apartheid;
> (k) Other inhumane acts of a similar character intentionally causing great suffering, or serious injury to body or to mental or physical health.

Notice both that sections (a)–(k) involve violations of human rights and that a crime against humanity can occur only if "committed as part of a widespread or systematic attack." And because the alternative account I have outlined here suggests that it is enough that human rights violations be either widespread or systematic (i.e., they need not be part of a single "attack"), this theory actually allows more normative room for international criminal law than the prevailing view.[13]

Given the substantial overlap between my recommendation and that of the International Criminal Court, one might think that we have little practical reason to revise the traditional conception of international criminal law. After all, even if I am correct that the category of crimes against humanity is both confused and unnecessary, at least it has been defined so as to capture the vast majority of the cases in which international criminal law would in fact be permissible. Thus, both because the category is so deeply entrenched and because its definition comes acceptably close to what a more theoretically defensible account would recommend, as a practical matter it might seem unwise to abandon it.

Because international criminal law is in a nascent and fragile state, it might well be best if we did not immediately try to dramatically revise the prevailing view. It is important to appreciate, however, that there remain compelling practical reasons to move beyond the category of crimes against humanity. The crucial point is that, just as Bentham famously worried that talk of natural rights was "pernicious nonsense" (insofar as such talk was not merely confused, it led people to support the wrong social institutions), talk of crimes against humanity is not merely conceptually ill-founded; in the long run it will undermine our best efforts to institute an effective system of international criminal law. This is because using the category of crimes against humanity implicitly endorses the Westphalian outlook, according to which each de facto state is entitled to unbridled sovereignty over its self-regarding affairs. And as long as we continue to trade in the currency of this Westphalian worldview, we lend credence to rogue leaders like Milosevic who protest that their international criminal prosecution is entirely unjustified.

The most important point of this section is that international criminal law may permissibly be imposed wherever widespread or systematic human rights violations are going unpunished, whether or not these violations have a border-crossing element. And the longer we continue to prosecute political and military leaders under the banner of crimes against humanity, the more we entrench the misconception that this international criminal prosecution is permissible only because these leaders have not merely committed atrocities against their own constituents, they have somehow harmed all of us. Revising the traditional view of international criminal law is therefore of the utmost practical importance because doing so will aid efforts to transform the current world into one in which political and military leaders everywhere exhibit a greater respect for the basic rights of their constituents.

CONCLUSION

In the previous chapter I argued that the traditional theories of punishment all lead us astray, because each wrongly focuses on a general justifying aim rather than moral side constraints. However, when we turn our attention from the question "Why may wrongdoers permissibly be punished?" to the distinct question "Why is the state uniquely authorized to treat wrongdoers in this way?" the crucial benefits of a properly constructed criminal legal system are clearly relevant. If the arguments of this and the previous chapter are on target, then we should now conclude that (1) wrongdoers cannot righteously object to being punished because, in wronging others, they have forfeited their rights against this hard treatment, and that (2) the state violates no rights in assuming exclusive control over the punitive process only because it is uniquely capable of adequately realizing the morally significant aims that a system of punishment can achieve.

Chapter 4

Torts versus Crimes

The standard way to distinguish between torts and crimes is to allege that the latter are in some important sense distinctively "public." I think we must look elsewhere for a principled distinction, and in this chapter I argue that the crucial difference between tort and criminal law ought to map onto the distinction between rights infringements and rights violations. I believe that moral rights are central to both areas of law, but that tort law is an appropriate response to rights-related harms whereas criminal law is a fitting response to rights-related culpability.

This chapter is divided into four sections. First I explain my dissatisfaction with the public/private distinction and then recommend focusing instead on the difference between violating versus merely infringing a moral right. Next I respond to concerns that abandoning the public/private dichotomy will lead to unacceptable implications. In the third section, I explore whether victims must necessarily have control over the tort process and the state must preside over criminal matters. And finally, I consider whether states should abandon criminal law and focus their efforts exclusively on improving tort law.

MOVING BEYOND THE PUBLIC/PRIVATE DISTINCTION

In his excellent entry "Legal Punishment" in the Stanford Encyclopedia of Philosophy, R. A. Duff acknowledges that "it is notoriously difficult to give a clear and plausible account of the distinction between civil and criminal law, between 'private' and 'public' legal wrongs, whether our interest is in the analytical question of what the distinction amounts to, or in the normative question of which kinds of wrong should fall into which category." I begin with this quote not only because Duff concedes how difficult it has been for criminal lawyers to explain and justify the distinction between civil and criminal law but also because it is revealing that Duff takes for granted that the distinction between civil and criminal law must correspond to the distinction between private and public matters. I believe that criminal lawyers have wrestled endlessly with this distinction precisely because they have (wrongly) presumed that it must be cashed out in terms of private and public concerns, and in this section I suggest that the key to understanding the difference between torts and crimes is to appreciate the distinction between rights infringements and rights violations.

It is worth beginning by noting why the public/private distinction is so tempting. In particular, arguably the biggest difference between tort and criminal proceedings is the party who controls the process. Imagine, for instance, that Zofia maliciously breaks David's arm. If David wants to sue Zofia for damages, he is free to do so; and if he decides not to pursue the matter, no one may unilaterally do so in his stead. But while David can decide whether or not to sue Zofia, he lacks control over the punitive process. The state claims dominion over the criminal proceedings, and thus the authorities unilaterally decide whether or not to press charges against Zofia. Most important, the state may prosecute Zofia even if David would prefer that she not be held accountable, and the state may decide not to press charges against Zofia even if David desperately wants to see her brought to justice. But if David is given control over the tort proceedings, why may the state claim dominion over the criminal process?

The natural answer to this question is that, while certain acts are merely private wrongs that do not concern the larger community, other acts are public wrongs that harm more than merely the direct victim. When Zofia breaks David's arm, for instance, she clearly harms him (and thus there is nothing mysterious about David's right to sue for damages). But Zofia's act is more than merely a private wrong, according to this line of thought, because it harms the entire community. And if the community as a whole is harmed by certain acts, then presumably there is nothing wrong with the polity as a whole assuming control of the punitive processes regarding these acts.

If one believes that the community can be harmed by certain acts, then this would explain why those particular acts are public wrongs, whereas others are merely private wrongs (and thus should not be subject to state punishment). I worry about this line of argument, though, because I am not convinced that the community as a whole is necessarily harmed when Zofia maliciously breaks David's arm. As a fellow human being, I would certainly prefer that Zofia not treat David in this fashion, and as a fellow citizen, I may feel less comfortable knowing that I live among malicious arm-breakers like Zofia, but neither of these considerations seems to entail that my compatriots and I are harmed to such an extent that we now have an actionable interest in the punitive process. To put it bluntly, as much as David's fellow citizens might be disturbed by the fact that Zofia has broken David's arm, none of us seems harmed in the morally relevant sense, and so I fail to see why we as a group ought to have a decisive say over whether Zofia should be prosecuted for this act. (Of course, we might worry that suspects would routinely be wrongly punished and/or overpunished if victims were given unlimited discretion over punishment, but these concerns regarding wrongful punishment do not explain why David should lack control over whether Zofia is *prosecuted*.)

In response to these concerns, Duff recommends an alternative approach, according to which public wrongs are those that "properly concern" the political community as a whole. As he explains, crimes are "public wrongs, not because of some further injury that they do to 'the public', but because they are wrongs that properly concern 'the public', ie [*sic*] wrongs that properly concern us all as citizens."[1] As Duff notes, "adultery is still criminal, and occasionally prosecuted, in some American states; but to liberals it is *clearly* a private matter."[2] If Zofia had broken a promise to David and committed adultery, for instance, then we should regard this as a purely private wrong. That is, while David might be entitled to restitution, compensation, and/or an apology, these types of wrongs are not the proper concern of the community at large. We need not deny that breaking promises and committing adultery are wrong, we merely insist that the political community has no standing over these types of acts, and thus it has no right to unilaterally preside over the process that responds to them.

Duff's suggestion is promising, but we should accept it only if we can furnish both a compelling argument as to why we as a political community have standing over *any* wrongs and a clear explanation as to what things are properly our concern and what matters are not. Because Duff is (in my estimation) the most sophisticated criminal lawyer to give this matter his sustained attention, and because he has provided neither this argument nor this explanation, I have come to doubt that the tort/crime distinction can be explained in terms of private and public wrongs. Indeed, in the conclusion of a recent article, Duff stresses: "I have not tried here to offer some set of determinate master principles or criteria by which we can decide which wrongs should be criminal and which (only) tortious—I doubt that any such set of principles or criteria can be provided."[3] And given these doubts, Duff now urges us to conceive of the public domain as being determined procedurally, rather than substantively. As he puts it,

> we should not assume (as too many theorists tend to assume) that we can create a rational and properly limited system of criminal law only if we can articulate a single master principle, or set of principles, that provides substantive general criteria by which we can identify the kinds of conduct that are in principle criminalizable; the search for such a principle or set of principles is doomed to failure. . . . The question of which kinds of conduct constitute public wrongs is then a matter for public political deliberation, which might focus on whether the conduct in question is a public matter, or on whether and how it is wrong: given the plurality of values by which a liberal polity will define itself, we should expect to find similar plurality among the starting points for the processes of criminalization.[4]

Those of us attracted to the public/private distinction thus appear to face a dilemma. Either we must supply some type of substantive criteria that vindicates this distinction, or we must concede that political communities are free to draw the line between public and private wherever they want. And because, like Duff, I am unable to supply these criteria, I must embrace the second horn of the dilemma. But if a political society is free to criminalize any and all torts that it chooses, we appear unable to criticize any given criminal legal system for improperly concerning itself with purely private matters. And if this is right, we need to look elsewhere for principled reasons to refrain from criminalizing all torts. In my view, we should focus on the distinction between rights infringements and rights violations.

The distinction between rights infringements and violations is often explained in terms of Joel Feinberg's example of the stranded hiker:

> Suppose that you are on a backpacking trip in the high mountain country when an unanticipated blizzard strikes the area with such ferocity that your life is imperiled. Fortunately, you stumble onto an unoccupied cabin, locked and boarded up for the winter, clearly somebody else's private property. You smash in a window, enter, and huddle in a corner for three days until the storm abates. During this period you help yourself to your unknown benefactor's food supply and burn his wooden furniture in the fireplace to keep warm. Surely you are justified in doing all these things, and yet you have infringed the clear rights of another person.[5]

If one believes that the cabin owner's property right is perfectly general and absolute, then one would deny that the backpacker may permissibly break into the cabin, even in these dire circumstances. Most believe that Feinberg's backpacker acts permissibly, though, so we insist that the backpacker has no duty to refrain from entering the cabin without the owner's permission in this case, because the backpacker's perilous circumstances override the cabin owner's right. The backpacker may incur a special, remedial obligation to compensate the cabin owner for any damage done, but as long as she makes the cabin owner whole, she violates no duties.

Contrast Feinberg's Backpacker with a malicious Vandal who breaks into the cabin, helps herself to some food and then burns some of the wooden furniture merely for the thrill of wantonly destroying someone else's property. Vandal clearly acts impermissibly. She may not owe any more compensation to the cabin owner than Backpacker would, but there is an important moral difference between these two insofar as Backpacker permissibly transgresses the cabin owner's property rights whereas Vandal does so impermissibly. Following Judith Thomson and Joel Feinberg, it is now standard to say that Backpacker merely *infringes* the cabin owner's rights whereas Vandal *violates* these rights.[6]

I should acknowledge that not everyone is comfortable with this distinction. John Oberdiek, for instance, has voiced the following concern about Thomson's account:

> What does the violation of a right call for that is distinctive from what is called for by the negative residue left by the (mere) infringement of a right? It seems that on Thomson's account, every bit of reactive currency is used to redress right infringements, leaving nothing more for right violations. If total compensation is owed for a right infringement, after all, there is by definition no more *compensation* that can be given in the morally more significant case of a right violation.
>
> Presumably, by Thomson's lights, far more moral residue lingers after someone's rights have been violated than after someone's rights have been infringed—infringements but not violations are permissible, after all. On Thomson's own view, it would seem, this fact should be reflected in the response that is warranted by each kind of case. However, Thomson pulls out all the stops for mere right infringements. Thomson does this in the Cabin Case, for she maintains that the cabin owner is due full compensation.[7]

In response to Oberdiek, I would counter that, even if we follow Thomson in suggesting that Vandal owes the cabin owner no more compensation than Backpacker, the distinction between rights infringements and violations is morally significant, because only Vandal is morally liable to punishment. In my view, those who infringe or violate rights may become civilly liable, but only rights violators are criminally liable.[8] As a consequence, a typical hiker who transgresses no rights is neither civilly nor criminally liable, an imperiled hiker who permissibly transgresses a right may become civilly but not criminally liable, and a malicious hiker who impermissibly transgresses a right may become both civilly and criminally liable.

The crucial idea here is that those who merely infringe rights do nothing wrong and thus do not forfeit their rights against being punished. Only rights violators forfeit their rights against being punished, and therefore it would be impermissible to punish anyone who did not (at least attempt to) violate someone else's rights. Those who infringe rights may permissibly be forced to make their victims whole, but only rights violators may permissibly be punished.[9] If this is correct, then there is a principled distinction between tort and criminal law, but it does not rest on a public/private distinction. It maps onto the difference between rights infringements and rights violations.

Given that rights violations are a proper subset of rights transgressions, it might appear that crimes are a subset of torts. This is not so, however, because neither all nor only rights violators forfeit their rights against punishment. Not all rights violators may permissibly be punished because, even though all rights violations are (by definition) unjustified, some are excused. If I break into your cabin and burn your furniture only because one of your enemies credibly threatens to harm my children unless I vandalize your property, for instance, then the duress under which I acted would excuse my violating your rights. Because (fully) excused actors have not forfeited their rights against punishment, I may not permissibly be punished despite the fact that I violated your rights. And if one believes (as I do) that those who fail in their attempts to violate the rights of others forfeit their rights against being punished, then it follows that not only rights violators may permissibly be punished. Imagine, for example, that my malicious attempt to burn down your cabin fails because the water (which I mistook for gasoline) with which I doused your cabin prevents my match from igniting the wood. In this case, I am morally liable to punishment even though I have neither violated your rights nor harmed you. As the cases of failed attempts and excused rights violations illustrate, it is a bit misleading to say that criminal law covers rights violations. More accurately, we should say that criminal law is the appropriate response to *rights-related culpability*.[10]

Putting all of this together, I submit that tort law is an appropriate response to rights-related harms, and criminal law is an appropriate response to rights-related culpability.[11] Because most rights violations are both harmful and unexcused, there is obviously a huge overlap between these two domains. But because many attempted rights violations are harmlessly committed by a culpable agent, there will be some acts that render agents criminally but not civilly liable. And because there will be many harmful rights infringements and excused rights violations, there will be some acts that render agents civilly but not criminally liable. But whether an act is the proper concern of civil and/or criminal law will depend upon the presence or absence of harm and culpability, not whether the act is public or private.

CONCERNS ABOUT ABANDONING THE PUBLIC/PRIVATE DISTINCTION

Even if one grants that the distinction between rights infringements and violations is conceptually plausible and morally significant, one might worry that eschewing the public/private distinction leads to unpalatable implications. Focusing exclusively on the distinction between rights infringements and violations appears to leave me unable to explain why it is necessarily impermissible for the state to criminally prosecute and punish people for violating quintessentially private rights or de minimis infractions, for instance. And conceiving of criminal law as a response to culpability would seem to leave no room for strict liability. I addressed some of these worries in chapter 2, but it is worth retracing my reasoning here in light of the more specific concern that my understanding of criminal law is under- and/or overinclusive.

To begin, let me concede that I have a fair bit of pretheoretic sympathy for the widespread presumption that certain matters are strictly private and that the state would be objectionably intrusive if it inserted itself into these arenas. Suppose, for instance, that, after promising Jane, his wife, that he will not engage in extramarital sexual relations, Joe commits adultery. As much as I might condemn Joe for his infidelity, this matter simply seems none of the state's business; it seems like the state would be violating Joe's and Jane's rights if it criminally prosecuted Joe for committing adultery. But notice: given that I have abandoned the public/private distinction, it is not clear how I can defend such a stance. On the contrary, in light of my conclusion that the criminal law may preside over all rights-related culpability and the fact that Joe culpably violated Jane's right to sexual monogamy, it seems to follow straightforwardly that the state may permissibly punish Joe for his infidelity.

One sensible response to this challenge is to stipulate that rights-related culpability is necessary but not sufficient for the permissibility of state punishment. It seems implausible to suppose that one cannot forfeit one's rights against punishment unless one culpably violates a "public" right, because this would imply not only that the state may not punish Joe for his infidelity but also that Jane has no right to do so. A more promising approach, then, would be to insist more specifically that *the state* may permissibly punish only violators of public rights. Most important, if there is a good argument for this position, there is no reason to suppose that it must be incompatible with forfeiture theory. Things become more interesting, however, because no one has supplied such an argument. (As noted above, Duff concedes that "It is notoriously difficult to give a clear and plausible account of the distinction between civil and criminal law, between 'private' and 'public' legal wrongs, whether our interest is in the analytical question of what the distinction amounts to, or in the normative question of which kinds of wrong should fall into which category.") And in the absence of an adequate argument, it is unclear why forfeiture theorists should be uniquely open to criticism for relying on intuition on this point. In other words, if the considered conviction that the state has principled reasons to keep out of certain private spheres is so widespread and deep-seated that leading theorists may openly assume this point without argument, then why should forfeiture theorists be embarrassed about following suit? In sum, whether or not there is a compelling argument that explains and justifies the public/private distinction, a rights forfeiture theorist is just as entitled as anyone to insist that the state has principled reasons to refrain from criminally pursuing citizens when they commit purely private wrongs.

Even so (and despite my pretheoretic attraction to the idea that some rights violations are distinctively private), I have come around to the view that there are at most only *practical* reasons to keep the state out of certain rights violations. My views have shifted because of my reflections on the case of Joe's physically beating Jane. If Joe batters his wife, then I have no qualms with the state criminally prosecuting and punishing him. I am utterly unmoved by the thought that the government would violate either Joe's or Jane's rights if it decided (against Jane's protests) to punish Joe for beating Jane. Even if Jane and Joe both preferred that the state not intervene, I do not believe that the state's criminal prosecution constitutes an unwarranted invasion into Jane's and Joe's private affairs. And, importantly, I am more confident that the state does no wrong in intervening in the battery case than I am that the state wrongly invades privacy in the adultery case. And because I can find no way (other than my pretheoretic intuitions) to distinguish between these two cases, the desire for a consistent account combined with my greater confidence that the state acts permissibly when it intervenes in the battery case has led me to revise my stance regarding the adultery case. As a consequence, while I remain open to the possibility that there may be (morally relevant) compelling *practical* reasons why we do not want our criminal legal institutions involved in the most intimate areas of our lives, I am comfortable with the conclusion that the state is at least in principle permitted to prosecute and punish all rights-related culpability.[12]

Against this, one might appeal to the strength of our intuitions as sufficient reason to reject the urge for consistency between the battery and adultery cases. This is a reasonable position. After all, consistency does not require treating all cases alike; more modestly, it requires only that we treat *like* cases alike, and our intuitions regarding these scenarios provides at least some evidence that the battery and adultery cases are morally distinct. I cannot (nor do I feel a pressing need to) conclusively defeat this line of thinking, but I would point out that there was a time relatively recently when "we" took ourselves to have principled reasons against interfering in what we regarded as private familial matters when a husband battered his wife and children or raped his wife. And given how terribly wrong "we" have been about the public/private distinction in the past, I am reluctant to be as trusting as I might otherwise be about our current intuitions in this area. Thus, while I have no strong objections against a rights forfeiture view that stipulates that the state may permissibly punish only those who violate "public" rights, I remain skeptical that there are distinctively private rights that the state has principled reasons to refrain from adjudicating. As a consequence, I am unmoved by the worry that my reliance upon the infringe/violate distinction renders me unable to explain why the state may not punish putatively "private" rights violations.

A second concern about my reliance on the infringement/violation distinction is that I appear unable to explain why the state must refrain from punishing de minimis offenses, crimes that are only trivially harmful. Virtually everyone takes for granted that the state should not prosecute (let alone punish) someone for stealing a potato chip off a friend's lunch plate, for instance. But because stealing a potato chip seems to be a paradigmatic rights violation, my account appears unable to explain why the state may not punish a chip thief. Given this awkward implication, my view must be rejected.

As I indicated in chapter 2, there is no reason to deny that the violators of relatively inconsequential rights forfeit their rights against correspondingly minimal punishments. I also believe that, if the state has reasons to refrain from punishing de minimis offenders, these reasons are practical rather than principled.

The claim that the state has merely practical reasons against concerning itself with de minimis offenses is confirmed by the fact that de minimis is a doctrine about the law in general, not about punishment in particular. The full expression of de minimis is *de minimis non curat lex,* which is commonly translated as "the law does not care for small things." The idea here is straightforward: Law is an expensive resource, so it is not worth the costs of utilizing it for trivial matters. And when it comes to criminal law, this general insight gives rise to moral reasons for the state to refrain from punishing insignificant rights violations. This is because, having been guided by the idea that law should not be concerned with trifling matters, we have designed institutions that equip prosecuting attorneys with only relatively severe punitive options. And given that prosecuting attorneys have only these blunt utensils at their disposal, it would flout the principle of proportionality for the authorities to exercise these harsh punitive measures against the violators of trivial rights. As Douglas Husak puts it, "when wrongdoing is utterly trivial, *no* criminal sanction—not even a suspended sentence—can be proportionate to it. Any amount of state punishment, no matter how lenient, imposes greater stigma on defendants than they deserve and is disproportionate to the seriousness of their offence. If so, a theory of criminal law that takes proportionality seriously has reason to afford exculpatory significance to de minimis."[13]

Perhaps unlike Husak, I believe that if we wanted to, there would be no principled reason that we could not expand the range of options available to our prosecuting attorneys so that they had very minor punishments that would fit such trivial rights violations. But because we recognize that giving officials these options is not worth the costs involved, we have practical reasons to refrain from doing so. In sum, I agree that existing states should not prosecute and punish de minimis offenders, but this is only because of the contingent fact that we have (for excellent practical reasons) not given our legal officials the tools with which to proportionately punish violators of relatively inconsequential rights.

Finally, let me briefly respond to the potential worry that conceiving of criminal law as a response to rights-related culpability bars me from accepting any strict liability statutes. This concern appears warranted: Given that strict liability is consistent with punishing someone who is in no way culpable, it is incompatible with my insistence that one cannot forfeit one's right against punishment without acting culpably.[14] As with the first two potential objections, however, this is a conclusion from which I do not shrink. I have always thought it unjust to impose strict liability criminal offenses, so I regard it as a virtue of my approach that it prohibits them on principled grounds. Of course, because I believe that the right against being punished (like all moral rights) is not absolute, I cannot antecedently rule out the possibility that a political community's dire circumstances might override an innocent person's right against being punished, but it is important to recognize that (1) this would be an exceptional case where an important moral right is outweighed only because of the grave stakes involved, and (2) this concession does not justify anything like the status quo, in which states far too frequently (in my view) resort to strict liability criminal offenses when such legislation appears to be the most convenient way to address a problem. In the end, then, just as I openly acknowledge that my account of criminal law cannot necessarily rule out the permissibility of punishing those who violate what appear to be trivial or purely private rights, I accept that my approach is incompatible with strict liability. These conclusions do not strike me as concessions, however, because I am not convinced that there are principled reasons why criminal law may not permissibly preside over de minimis or putatively private matters, and I have no qualms insisting that we should refrain from enforcing strict liability criminal statutes.

STATE VERSUS INDIVIDUAL DISCRETION

Another question that arises once we jettison the public/private distinction is why tort cases may be initiated by the plaintiff whereas criminal cases must be brought by the state as a whole. If the crucial element required for criminal prosecution is simply that a right is violated rather than merely infringed, then why may the victim not have discretion over both the civil and criminal proceedings? There might be several types of crimes (like espionage or pollution, for instance) where the state seems uniquely suited to exercise control, but in most instances it is unclear why we should not defer to the individual whose rights have been violated.

To appreciate the force of this question, recall the cabin owner from Feinberg's example. When the malicious Vandal breaks into the cabin and burns some of the furniture, the cabin owner is in a position to claim or waive his right to compensation. But if there is no inherently public element to Vandal's act, why does the state as a whole get to decide whether this Vandal is criminally prosecuted? Put another way: Given that rights violations appear no more public than rights infringements, why does the cabin owner not also have discretion as to whether or not to press criminal charges?

How a forfeiture theorist answers this question may hinge on whether she thinks the right to punish in the state of nature is competitive or exclusive. If one thinks that the right to punish is competitive, one can appeal to a moral principle that explains why the state as a whole should have dominion over the criminal legal process. But if one thinks that the right to punish in the state of nature is exclusive, one can supply only practical considerations in support of this difference between civil and criminal proceedings.

As I noted in chapter 3, I follow most rights forfeiture theorists in believing that the person whose right was violated enjoys an exclusive right to compensation but only a competitive right to punish. And if only the victim is in a position to claim compensation, she has the moral power to unilaterally waive this right. But because *anyone* is morally entitled to punish a rights violator, the victim cannot unilaterally waive this right; otherwise, she would have the power to waive the rights of others. By comparison, imagine that the United States borrows $1 trillion from China. In a case such as this, an average Chinese citizen does not have the moral power to waive the right to repayment. It is possible for this right to be waived, but given that this debt is owed to the Chinese as a group, only the appropriate political representatives have the requisite standing to forgive this debt. And if there is a competitive right to punish, it stands to reason that only the appropriate political officials would have the standing to waive the right to punish.

For those inclined to posit a competitive right to punish, this response seems straightforward and compelling. Even so, at least two questions remain. First and most obviously, as I acknowledged in chapter 3, reasonable people can disagree about whether the right to punish in the state of nature is competitive or exclusive. And if there are no decisive grounds with which we can rule out the plausibility of an exclusive right to punish, it is not clear how confident we should be in a putatively principled justification for a fundamental difference between tort and criminal law that presupposes the presence of a competitive right to punish.

Second, one might worry that my initial inclination to endorse the competitive right to punish covertly smuggles in the private/public distinction that I have now renounced. To see why this is the case, recall that my attraction to the competitive right to punish arose from what I regard as two problems with conceiving of the right to punish as an exclusive right. The first (and less important) issue arises when one person kills another. In this case, I worried that if the victim enjoys an exclusive right to punish the rights violator, then the murderer may not permissibly be punished because the only person who would have had the standing to do so is now dead. I admit that this objection is relatively minor, however, because it does not seem too great of a stretch to suppose that the right to punish might be extended to the victim's survivors in a case like this. My second reservation about positing an exclusive right to punish stemmed from its implication that victims would then have the right to effectively pardon rights violators. And because I am inclined to think that third parties may permissibly punish a wrongdoer even when the victim wants to waive her right to punish, I was averse to the idea that victims have the moral power to unilaterally pardon those who have violated their rights. But notice: if rights violations are in no morally relevant sense public, then why should I resist the idea that the victim has the right to unilaterally pardon the wrongdoer? If I am really going to distance myself from authors like Duff who allege that some wrongs "properly concern all of us as citizens," then on what grounds can I suggest that third parties retain a right to punish a rights violator when the victim genuinely prefers that the person who wronged her not be punished? We take it for granted that no third party may permissibly force the United States to pay

China $1 trillion if China has forgiven this debt, so if rights violations are strictly private matters, perhaps it follows that third parties may not punish wrongdoers without the permission of the person who was wronged. Viewed in this light, my central motivation for embracing the competitive right to punish may not fit comfortably with my rejection of the notion that crimes are somehow inherently public. Indeed, my preference for a competitive right to punish may simply be one particular instantiation of my more general pretheoretic inclination to accept the public/private distinction. If so, then it certainly seems objectionable for me to reject the public/private distinction for lack of an argument in its support and yet continue to invoke my belief in the competitive right to punish as a premise in an argument for how the criminal legal institutions should be organized.

One potential way to counter the allegation that belief in the competitive right to punish presupposes the validity of the public/private distinction is to explore the permissibility of unrelated third parties punishing adulterers in the state of nature. If one believes that some random individual, Julie, violates no rights if she proportionately punishes Joe in the state of nature for his lack of fidelity to Jane, then it seems clear that one's support for the competitive right to punish is compatible with renouncing the public/private distinction. If one believes that Julie has the right to punish Joe for breaking Jane's arm but may not permissibly punish him for committing adultery, however, then this lends credence to the worry that theorists like me endorse the competitive right to punish only because we (perhaps unconsciously) presume that the public/private distinction is valid. For my purposes, it would be convenient if I could report complete confidence in the judgment that Julie may permissibly punish Joe for adultery in the state of nature. I must confess, however, that this is not so. I am not sure that it is necessarily *im*permissible for Julie to punish Joe for his lack of fidelity, but I am certainly less confident that she may punish Joe for adultery than I am that she may punish him for breaking Jane's arm.

An alternative explanation for the competitive nature of the right to punish invokes retributivism. The retributivist's concern with desert may be helpful, because desert does not seem relational in the same way as compensation. To see this, recall the earlier example in which Vandal breaks into the cabin and burns some of the furniture. As a rights forfeiture theorist with (mild) retributivist leanings, I believe that (1) Vandal has forfeited her right against proportionate punishment, (2) Vandal owes compensation to the cabin owner, and (3) Vandal deserves to be proportionately punished. Focusing on (2) and (3), notice that the compensation is relational in a way the desert is not because the former is *owed to* the cabin owner, whereas the latter is not. (Theorists sometimes suggest that punishment is "owed to" the Vandal rather than the cabin owner, but this expression has always struck me as, at best, misleading because, if punishment was owed to Vandal in the same way that compensation is owed to the cabin owner, Vandal could simply waive her claim to punishment.) This explains why, even if the cabin owner may claim or waive her right to compensation, her preferences do not similarly determine whether the Vandal deserves punishment (and whether others may permissibly punish her). And if so, this might explain why the right to punish is competitive. Since there is nothing about rights forfeiture theory that requires one to endorse retributivism, there is room for forfeiture theorists to disagree about desert (and thereby to disagree whether the right to punish is competitive). Importantly, though, forfeiture theorists who happen also to be retributivists (as I am) can insist that the right to punish is competitive without committing themselves to the notion that a subset of rights violations are somehow distinctively public.

Importantly, though, some forfeiture theorists might (not unreasonably) both (1) understand the right to punish to be held exclusively by the victim and (2) eschew retributivism. Theorists of this stripe appear unable to furnish principled reasons why tort cases should be under the control of the plaintiff while criminal proceedings should be initiated at the discretion of the state as a whole. Given this, it is worth considering whether there are practical considerations that count in favor of these common practices. In this vein, it is tempting to suppose that public officials must control the punitive process, because the victims themselves would routinely punish the innocent and overpunish the guilty. This answer will not justify the difference between tort and criminal law, however, because we do not allow plaintiffs to unilaterally decide whether or not their defendants are civilly liable and, if so, how much compensation the latter must pay. More minimally, we allow the person whose right was transgressed to decide only whether or not to sue the defendant, and then the state as a whole decides how the case should be resolved. And since giving the victim similar discretion as to whether or not the defendant should be criminally prosecuted would not lead straightforwardly to mass wrongful or overpunishment if the state continued to preside over the trials, sentencings, and punishments, our standard justification for state control over the process would not seem to answer the question on which I am currently focused.

Indeed, if anything, the opposite might be the case; we want the state to decide whether to initiate prosecutions in order to avoid problematic *under*punishment. The reasoning here is as follows: We need states in order to protect our basic human rights; states can do this only if they adequately deter crime; they can deter crime only if a sufficient proportion of criminals are punished; an adequate proportion will be punished only if a satisfactory number are prosecuted; and finally, an adequate proportion will not be prosecuted if the victims themselves are given exclusive control over whether to press charges.

The key premise in this chain of reasoning is the (contestable) empirical claim that victims would not choose to prosecute enough.

Why think this, especially when we have no such worries about civil complaints? Here two differences seem salient. First, as much as those of us concerned with efficiency might worry about too few tort cases, we should be more concerned with underpunishment, since the proportion of punishment would clearly seem to play a greater role in deterrence than the proportion of civil suits. Second, although folks regularly speak of the punishment restoring the victim, the restoration is typically more metaphorical than real. Because of this, victims are often less motivated to seek punishment than to pursue financial compensation. Put bluntly, given the twin facts that (1) a wrongdoer's conviction results in no monetary compensation for the victim, and (2) one criminal's conviction will typically make only a negligible difference to deterring other potential criminals, it is not unreasonable to worry that many victims would prefer not to take the time and energy to press charges.[15] If so, we appear to have a clear instance of a collective action problem, wherein everyone recognizes that we would all be better off if more victims pressed charges against those who wronged them, but each victim has insufficient incentive to do so in her particular case. And just as we utilize the state to solve a variety of other collective action problems, it seems prudent to appoint prosecuting attorneys who are assigned the chore of pressing criminal charges against defendants whenever the evidence warrants, whether or not the victims themselves are enthusiastic about these particular prosecutions.

To review: if there is an exclusive right to compensation but a competitive right to punish, this provides a principled explanation for why plaintiffs should be allowed to decide whether to initiate tort cases while the state as a whole ought to decide whether a defendant is criminally prosecuted. If there is an exclusive right to punish, however, then we begin with a presumption in favor of allowing the victim to control both processes. This presumption stands in the civil arena, but it is defeated within criminal law by the weighty practical concern that victim dominion over criminal prosecution would ultimately result in insufficient punishment to adequately deter rights violations.

WHY NOT ABANDON CRIMINAL LAW?

In his influential article "Restitution: A New Paradigm of Criminal Justice," Randy Barnett argues against retributivism and in favor of restitution. It is worth pausing to engage with Barnett's argument because he, too, believes that crimes are entirely private. The lesson he draws from this conclusion, though, is that we should abandon state punishment altogether. Let us examine his argument, then, to see whether denying the public element of crimes strips us of any motivation and/or justification for a criminal legal system.

Barnett derives his paradigm of restitution from the private nature of crimes as follows: "The idea of restitution is actually quite simple. It views crime as an offense by one individual against another. The victim has suffered a loss. Justice consists of the culpable offender making good the loss he has caused. It calls for a complete refocusing of our image of crime. . . . Where we once saw an offense against society, we now see an offense against an individual victim. . . . The armed robber did not rob society; he robbed the victim. His debt, therefore, is not to society; it is to the victim."[16] Given this characterization, it is not surprising that Barnett would urge us to focus on making the victim whole. Barnett's reasoning is particularly interesting because he does not merely suggest that restoring the victim should be our foremost priority; he alleges that this should be our *exclusive* concern. The pivotal idea here is that, because the robber robs only his victim, our sole postcrime aim should be to restore the victim to her ex ante position. If society had also been robbed (or otherwise harmed) by the wrongdoer, then we might have to do more to make things right.

But because the rights violation is a purely private affair between the wrongdoer and her victim, our work is complete once the victim has been made whole. But if this is right, there is no need to punish anyone. In other words, as long as we have an effective system of civil law, we have no need (or justification) for a criminal legal system.

Not surprisingly, Barnett's provocative analysis has garnered a number of prominent responses.[17] Franklin G. Miller, for example, worries that civil law does not provide an effective venue for society to express its core values. As he puts it, "before we choose to reject the paradigm of punishment in favor of the paradigm of restitution, we need to consider what might be lost as a result. Could a system of pure restitution preserve this condemnatory aspect of punishment? If not, is this something that we should be willing to give up?"[18]

For several reasons, I suspect that the expressivist's reply will not suffice. First of all, it is not clear why officials within the civil legal system cannot explicitly communicate society's core values. Why can they not distinguish between rights infringers and rights violators, for instance, and explicitly condemn only the latter? Indeed, I think there is an important sense in which restitution might enable public officials to *better* capture the desired condemnatory message, because it conveys that the offender did something wrong by violating *the victim's rights*, which is principally what we want to convey (rather than that the criminal disrespected *our values*). Against this, Miller might counter that values are best expressed through action rather than mere words. Even if this is true, however, it is not clear that punishment is the only (or even the best) way for a society to demonstrate its values. For the sake of argument, though, let us concede that there is no better way to convey one's values (or at least these types of values) than by meting out hard treatment to those who flout them. Even so, would this aim be important enough to justify taxing citizens in order to fund an expensive criminal legal system? In my view, Victor Tadros is correct to conclude that the "communicative goal of punishment would need to be supplemented by other goals to justify a system of state punishment, or any systematic punitive institutions."[19]

Arguing from a retributivist perspective, Roger Pilon raises a second worry about Barnett's analysis, and, importantly, he articulates this objection without suggesting that there is anything inherently public about crimes. Pilon writes: "If a rich man rapes a rich woman, are we really to suppose that monetary damages will restore the status quo, will satisfy the claims of justice? A wealthy child molester will treat compensation simply as the price of pleasure! And what of the terrorist who murders, knowing that his wealthy backer will settle the account? The reduction of criminal wrongs to civil wrongs, in short, or at least the addressing of criminal wrongs with civil remedies, bespeaks an all too primitive view of what in fact is at issue in the matter of crime."[20] I share these concerns. Like Pilon, I shudder at the thought of a legal system in which someone like the Marquis de Sade might be permitted merely to give money to those he wrongs and then (because of his wealth) be allowed to continue violating the rights of others. Put simply, I believe a world in which the virtuous flourish and wrongdoers are punished is morally preferable to one in which both flourish. I must concede, however, that (other than thought experiments like those involving the Marquis de Sade) I have no argument to support my retributivist inclinations against sophisticated critics like Tadros. Even if I did, though, I agree with Tadros that merely giving wrongdoers what they deserve would not justify state punishment.[21]

To see that the retributive aims on their own (i.e., when isolated from our concern to deter prospective criminals) is not sufficiently important, imagine a world in which retributivism and deterrence are disentangled because rights-related culpability is perfectly correlated with incompetence, so that every attempt to violate a right invariably fails. Under these circumstances, we have no reason to fear potential criminals, because those able to commit crimes would lack the inclination to do so, while those inclined to wrong others would be unable to successfully do so. A criminal legal system in this case would concern itself solely with punishing failed attempts. As a forfeiture theorist who maintains both that (1) rights-related culpability is sufficient to forfeit one's right against punishment and that (2) retributivists are correct that we have moral reasons to punish culpability, I believe that we have moral reasons to set up a criminal legal system in this imaginary world. What I deny, though, is that these reasons are weighty enough to justify state coercion. Achieving retributive justice strikes me as the most compelling nondeterrent reason to create a criminal legal system, so I might well create and sustain such a system if I could do so by merely snapping my fingers. In the real world, though, criminal law is an extremely costly enterprise that can only feasibly be supported through taxation. Thus, even if we fantasized about an ideal system (which neither expanded beyond its legitimate proportions nor wrongly punished the innocent or overpunished the guilty), ensuring that wrongdoers receive the punishment they deserve is not important enough to justify taxation.[22]

This thought experiment in which all potential criminals are incompetent confirms that our chief interest in criminal law is deterrence, rather than expressivism, retributivism or any other aim. In my view, the only reason compelling enough to justify a state system of criminal law is that, in addition to civil remedies, we want a "kicker" to help deter crime.[23] The paramount function states perform is protecting the human rights of their constituents, and they could not do this without deterring prospective rights violators with the threat of punishment. In addition to restoring victims, we want to minimize the number of future victims. And performing this task, I submit, is important enough to justify taxing citizens to create a criminal legal system. It bears noting, though, that this argument relies on the empirical premise that the threat of punishment is both necessary and sufficient to adequately deter crime. If the threat of punishment did not provide a sufficiently robust marginal deterrent effect (either because potential criminals were unmoved by the fear of punishment or because a sufficient number were already effectively deterred by civil law), then I would join Barnett in suggesting that we should abandon criminal law and focus exclusively on doing all we can to ensure that rights violators restore their victims.[24]

Against this, one might protest that victims are entitled to see that those who wronged them are punished. The idea here is that, even if in the move from the state of nature to a legitimate state the victim loses her right to *personally* punish her rights violator, she at least retains the right to see that this criminal is punished. So if the state prohibits vigilante justice, it thereby incurs a duty to punish rights violators on behalf of the victims.

This may be correct, but I would caution that the victim's right to see that her rights violator is punished is merely presumptive, and thus is vulnerable to being overridden in extenuating circumstances. To see that this is so, think of the South African Truth and Reconciliation Commission. In the wake of apartheid, South African officials (reasonably) worried that an attempt to pursue retributive justice against all rights violators within the previous regime would not only be terribly expensive (if not practically impossible), it would impede the transition toward a peaceful and just society. Based on this reasoning, officials who perpetrated injustices during apartheid were given immunity from criminal punishment for their political actions if they publicly confessed to their wrongdoing. Rights violators could still be held civilly liable (and the Truth and Reconciliation Commission's criminal immunity did not extend to personal—i.e., nonpolitical—wrongs), but masses of government officials who would ordinarily have been subjected to severe criminal punishment were pardoned.

Given how dramatically the Truth and Reconciliation Commission diverged from standard criminal legal practice, it is not surprising that it was met with a wide variety of criticisms. The most important for my purposes, though, is that pardoning all of these officials violated the rights of victims to see their wrongdoers punished. This strikes me as a reasonable complaint. Just as I believe that each of us in the state of nature has a (presumptive) right to personally punish those who have wronged us, one might think that all of us in a legitimate state have a (defeasible) right that the state criminally prosecute and punish those who have violated our rights.[25] Notice, though: Just as an individual's right to personally punish can be outweighed by the urgent need for law and order, the more general right to have one's wrongdoer punished can be outweighed if this is necessary for peace and prosperity. Both in the move from the state of nature to a legitimate state and in the transition from an illegitimate to a legitimate regime, the urgency of establishing a just and peaceful society explains why presumptive individual rights are overridden. Thus, if defenders of the Truth and Reconciliation Commission were correct to speculate that departing radically from retributive justice was necessary to graduate to a peaceful and prosperous future, then this practice was fully justified, despite the presence of competing individual rights to see one's wrongdoers punished.

Assuming that the Truth and Reconciliation Commission's departure from standard criminal law was permissible, it is worth considering whether this lesson can be generalized. For example, would an average US citizen's rights be violated if the United States eliminated the criminal law (and prohibited vigilantism), if this reduced overall crime? Imagine, for instance, that the United States redirected the enormous funds it currently spends on criminal justice to education, preventative medicine, and fortifying the civil legal system. If I am right that the only sufficiently compelling justification for criminal law is that a government-run system of punishment is necessary to adequately deter crime, then it seems to follow straightforwardly that eliminating the US criminal legal system would not violate any rights if this could be done in a manner that resulted in fewer rights violations. I therefore conclude that Barnett's case against punishment can be defeated, but only on the (reasonable, I think) empirical assumption that states typically have no feasible way to satisfactorily protect the human rights of their constituents other than to assume monopolistic control over the criminal legal processes.[26]

CONCLUSION

Whatever else states might do, we want them to oversee systems of civil and criminal law, because we need governments to ensure that those who have been harmed by rights transgressions are made whole and that prospective wrongdoers are effectively deterred from violating the rights of others. We are correct to insist that legal officials wield more control over criminal than civil proceedings, but this is not because crimes are distinctively public wrongs. If there is a principled difference between torts and crimes, it correlates with the distinction between rights infringements and rights violations. Drawing upon this distinction, we can see that tort law is the appropriate response to rights-related harms, while criminal law is the proper response to rights-related culpability.

Chapter 5

Procedural Rights

One important question for rights forfeiture theorists is whether a wrongdoer forfeits her right not to be punished as soon as she violates someone else's rights or only after she has been duly convicted of doing so. Before working on this subject, I would have insisted that procedural rights are nonnegotiable and thus that it would necessarily be impermissible to punish someone without first conclusively establishing her guilt via a fair, reliable, and public process. After reviewing the arguments in favor of procedural rights, however, I find myself unable to produce a satisfactory defense of my pretheoretic convictions. As a result, I now doubt that there is a general moral right to a fair trial, and in this chapter I defend the stark thesis that, absent special circumstances, there are no moral procedural rights.[1]

I divide this chapter into four main sections. First I argue that there is no general moral right against double jeopardy. Next I explain why punishing a wrongdoer without first establishing her guilt via a fair trial does not necessarily violate her rights. In the third section I respond to a number of possible objections. And finally, I consider the implications of my arguments for the human right to due process.

DOUBLE JEOPARDY

For two reasons, I begin by contesting the widespread presumption that we have a moral right against being prosecuted more than once for the same crime. First, given that it is generally accepted that there are many procedural rights, I must discuss more than the right to a fair and reliable trial if I want to defend the broader thesis that there are no preinstitutional procedural rights. Space considerations obviously do not allow me to analyze each potential procedural right separately, but if I can make parallel cases against two of the most widely affirmed procedural rights, this will at least lend credence to my more general skepticism regarding procedural rights as a whole. Second, even though the right against double jeopardy is commonly regarded as a core right, I suspect that there is less resistance to its denial than there would be to contesting the moral right to a fair trial. So, if I can first show that we have good reason to question the right against double jeopardy, this may render readers less resistant to the more radical conclusions to follow.

Given my view that there is no general moral right to be tried no more than once for any given crime, how do I explain the intuitive appeal of the prohibition against double jeopardy? I believe that we have good instrumental reasons to design our legal systems so that prosecutors know they can try someone only once for any given crime. Trials are extremely (financially and personally) costly, so we have obvious pragmatic reasons to keep them to a minimum. In addition, we should be concerned about a situation in which legal officials can continually harass citizens by repeatedly charging them for the same crime, or charging folks when there is very little evidence (since they could simply prosecute again later if the defendant is acquitted). In other words, in the absence of a strict prohibition against multiple jeopardy, there would be too much room for the authorities to abuse their powers, thereby undermining the citizens' capacities to lead good lives. And once legal institutions incorporate this prohibition, citizens have *legal* (though not necessarily moral) rights against double jeopardy.

But don't citizens also have a *moral* right against double jeopardy? Perhaps; but if so, it is not because this right is a preinstitutional moral right (like an innocent person's right not to be punished) that holds globally in the state of nature or any other institutional context. Rather, if contemporary citizens have a moral right against double jeopardy, I would think it is only because, *once the state has publicly announced that it will not try anyone twice for the same crime*, it thereby incurs a special duty to keep its word. What is more, while this duty is *regarding* the person who has already been tried once, it need not be especially *owed to* this person. Thus, it may be that the state's moral duty not to criminally prosecute Jane twice for a given crime is *regarding* Jane, but it is *owed to* all of the citizens equally (though Jane is of course likely to care the most that this duty is respected).

Moreover, even if we assume for now that one's guilt must be established via a fair and reliable procedure, it remains an open question whether we must avoid double jeopardy. This is because reliability is dual-faced, and only one of its faces recommends avoiding multiple jeopardy. More specifically, reliability cannot be understood solely in terms of avoiding the conviction of innocent defendants; otherwise, the most reliable procedure would just be to summarily acquit all suspects. Instead, a procedure is reliable to the extent that it maximizes the number of guilty people convicted and minimizes the number of innocent convicted. And while our concern to avoid wrongly convicting the innocent suggests that we should prohibit multiple jeopardy, our aim to convict as many guilty criminals as possible counts in favor of it. What is more, reasonable people can disagree about how to weigh the competing concerns of convicting the guilty and exonerating the innocent. Should we prefer a system wherein twenty out of a hundred guilty defendants are acquitted while two out of a hundred innocent people are wrongly convicted, or an alternative system in which thirty out of a hundred guilty defendants are acquitted but only one out of every hundred innocent people is wrongly convicted? It is not clear.

Even if one ratio were incontrovertibly better than another, though, this would not settle the question of double jeopardy, because it is possible that we could increase the percentage of guilty people convicted *and* decrease the number of innocent people wrongly convicted by allowing double jeopardy but increasing the burden of proof that the prosecution must establish. In that case, no one could complain that a criminal legal system was made less reliable when it was amended to allow double jeopardy. Most important, it is interesting to ask "Whose rights would be violated if a society moved from a system with a lower presumption required to establish guilt combined with a prohibition of multiple jeopardy to a system with a higher presumption of innocence and the possibility (in certain circumstances) for multiple jeopardy?" I submit that no one's rights would be violated. The basic point is that prohibiting double jeopardy may well make sense in certain (or even most) institutional contexts, but that does not mean that we are required as a matter of principle to avoid multiple jeopardy in all contexts. And if there are institutional arrangements that can be made more reliable by allowing double jeopardy, it does not seem that anyone's rights would necessarily be violated by allowing double jeopardy in those contexts.

Before closing this section, it is worth comparing double jeopardy to the statute of limitations in the criminal law, because I would urge us to conceive of the two in similar terms. There are a variety of good reasons to limit the period of time after a crime during which one may be prosecuted for it. Suppose that, in view of these reasons, Nora's jurisdiction enacts a statute of limitations that precludes the authorities from prosecuting crimes that were committed more than seven years earlier. In these circumstances, Nora presumably has a legal, and perhaps even a moral, right not to be prosecuted for an act that she may have committed more than seven years earlier. But one can acknowledge this without affirming the quite distinct claim that Nora has a preinstitutional moral right that no criminal legal system with jurisdiction over her be designed so as to prosecute crimes committed more than seven years earlier. If Nora's legal system had decided to place the statute of limitations at eight instead of seven years, for instance, it is hard to see how her moral rights would have been violated.

People are unlikely to think there is anything magical about the particular duration of seven years, so I presume that this much is relatively uncontroversial. In my view, though, we should reason similarly about single jeopardy. Although one is obviously a salient number, and the difference between being prosecuted once and being prosecuted twice for the same crime is in many ways more significant than the difference between being prosecuted for a crime one may have committed six years and 364 days earlier and being prosecuted for a crime one may have committed seven years and one day earlier, I suggest that there is no more magic in the number one than there is in the duration of seven years. In my view, those who design and regulate a legal system do not necessarily violate their constituents' moral rights when they move from single to multiple jeopardy any more than they do when they increase the criminal statute of limitations from seven to eight years or reduce the legal speed limit from sixty-five to fifty-five miles per hour along a given stretch of highway. I appreciate that there may be compelling practical reasons to prohibit prosecuting defendants more than once for the same crime (just as there might be good policy arguments in favor of higher speed limits or a shorter period of statute of limitations), but this is quite different from alleging that one's moral rights are necessarily violated if one is prosecuted more than once for the same crime.

FAIR, RELIABLE, AND PUBLIC PROCEDURES

I am inclined to understand the right to a fair trial just as I have analyzed double jeopardy: I think we have ample reason to insist that the state not punish anyone until she has been found guilty by an appropriate procedure, *not because each individual retains her right against being punished until she has been proven guilty by a fair, reliable, and public process,* but because we should take great care to minimize the number of people wrongly punished. In other words, we have instrumental, rather than intrinsic, reasons to design our judicial institutions in this way. If and when a criminal legal system is constructed along these lines, its constituents may well acquire a legal and moral right not to be punished before being found guilty, but this would merely be because those who operate the judicial system have a special duty to adhere to the publicly promulgated rules.

My position obviously flies in the face of the standard view that each of us has a preinstitutional right not to be punished until she has been duly convicted in a fair trial.[2] To vindicate my unorthodox view, I will construct an imaginary case in which this putative right is egregiously disrespected, and then I will argue that the person punished is not actually wronged.

Imagine that Sandra lives in a marvelous society appropriately called Justland. Justland is not entirely free of crime, but it enjoys an extremely low crime rate, and every single criminal in the history of Justland has been swiftly apprehended, duly convicted, and appropriately punished. Until recently, that is. Several months ago, someone stole a substantial sum of money from the state treasury. After an exhaustive investigation has turned up no leads, the prime minister proposes a wacky "solution" to close the books on this case: In light of their inability to apprehend the thief, why not simply hold a lottery and then punish the person whose name is drawn?[3] Given the radical nature of this proposal, the prime minister is reluctant to move forward with it unilaterally, so she holds a plebiscite on the issue. After extensive public discussion and deliberation, all 10 million Justlanders vote in the plebiscite, and the motion is affirmed by a two-thirds majority. The social security numbers of every citizen are then fed into a computer program that randomly selects Sandra's number. Everyone understands that Sandra is no more likely to be guilty than any of her 10 million compatriots, but in keeping with the verdict of the plebiscite, the authorities swiftly apprehend and duly punish Sandra. Finally, let me add just one more wrinkle: by a spectacular coincidence (and unbeknownst to any of the authorities who have apprehended and punished her), Sandra is the one who actually stole the money from the treasury.

Have any of Sandra's rights been violated? If one believes that there is a general moral right not to be punished unless one has been duly convicted by a fair and reliable process, then one should certainly think so. Insofar as having one's name drawn in a random lottery is a quintessentially unreliable way of establishing one's guilt, this would appear to be a paradigmatic instance of such a rights violation. In my view, however, no rights have been violated. In defense of this conclusion, let me juxtapose this case with two very similar scenarios in which I believe Sandra's moral rights *would* have been violated.

In the first variation, let us suppose that Sandra did not steal the money from the treasury. In this case, her right not to be subjected to the hard treatment of punishment has been violated. Given that Sandra is innocent, she has done nothing to forfeit this right, and the citizens of Justland cannot hide behind the fact that the lottery was democratically endorsed any more than they could justify enslaving Sandra on the grounds that society democratically voted to institute slavery. The crucial idea here is simple: whatever one thinks about the instrumental and/or intrinsic desirability of making collective decisions democratically, even democratic groups are constrained by individual moral rights. And because each of us has a weighty preinstitutional right not to be punished unless we have acted wrongly, Sandra can righteously object to her punishment even though the decision to hold the lottery was reached via a perfectly democratic process.

As a proponent of forfeiture theory, I am entirely sympathetic to this analysis. But this objection is obviously inapplicable to the original scenario in which Sandra stole the money from the treasury, because in that case she did forfeit her right not to be punished, and we cannot object that the Justlanders have violated Sandra's right not to be punished when she has clearly forfeited that right. (Of course, one might counter that Sandra forfeits her right against being punished only if and when she has been *duly convicted* of committing the crime, but this response begs the crucial question by presuming that there is an antecedent moral right to have one's guilt established by a fair and reliable process.) So while it is plausible to suppose that the punishment would have violated Sandra's rights if she were innocent, it does not appear that her rights were necessarily violated in the original case, where she was the one who stole the money from the treasury.

Second, it is important to distinguish our original scenario from one in which a society *routinely* uses a lottery to determine whom to punish. Imagine, for instance, that instead of voting to randomly select someone to be punished in only this one instance, the Justlanders voted to use the lottery for all crimes that were not solved within forty-eight hours. In a society that regularly selected people for state punishment in this fashion, a citizen's capacity to live a good life might well be undermined by the constant fear of being wrongly punished. In other words, even those whose names are not selected and thus are never punished will be wronged by being exposed to the risks of serious harm. Of course, none of us has a right to be sheltered from all risks, but we have rights against being exposed to unreasonable risks.[4] And because nothing substantial would be gained from instituting a policy of randomly selecting a person to be punished for any crime that is not solved within forty-eight hours, the risks of this practice seem patently unreasonable. Again, the mere fact that this policy was approved in a free and fair plebiscite is not enough to sanitize it of its moral impropriety, since the majority has no more of a right to expose innocent individuals to such grave and unnecessary risks than it does to enslave them. (In fact, if the punishments often involve incarceration, this practice seems morally tantamount to a democratically approved policy of enslaving randomly selected citizens.)

As with the first variation, I am receptive to this explanation of how moral rights would be violated in this scenario. And unlike in the first variation, this analysis appears to have implications for our original case. I say this because it seems plausible to suppose that even a single iteration of this type of lottery might be ruled out as a matter of principle insofar as it exposed folks to unreasonable risks. Presumably most people's lives will be much less affected if they are exposed to only one such lottery than if they had to awake each morning to learn if they (or any of their loved ones) have been selected in the daily lottery, but the mere fact that a single iteration of this type of lottery generates *less* risk does not show that these risks are *reasonable*. And because no such lottery would produce any significant benefits, the citizens of Justland could righteously object to the risks created by even the single lottery imagined in the original scenario. Thus, just as I violate the rights of everyone standing below when I chuck a grand piano off of a tall building, even if I throw only one piano and it hits only one person, each citizen of Justland (or at least each citizen who did not vote in favor of the plebiscite) would have her rights violated by the single use of the lottery, even though Sandra was the only one selected and punished. Those not hit by the piano and those not selected for punishment have their moral rights violated by being exposed to unreasonable risks of harms.

It is important to appreciate, however, that while this reasoning seems apt for virtually every citizen of Justland, it does not apply to Sandra in the original case. Given that Sandra is guilty of the crime in question, she has forfeited her right against being punished. And because she has no right against being punished, she lacks the standing to object to a policy that exposes her to a *risk* of being punished. To appreciate this point, imagine a variation on the piano case. Suppose that Ingrid is an adrenaline junky who asks me to throw a piano off of a tall building while she stands below, so that she can enjoy the extreme sport of piano-dodging. If I then throw this piano off of the building while a hundred unsuspecting bystanders are milling about below, it seems plausible to conclude that, while I have violated the rights of these other one hundred folks, I have done no wrong to Ingrid (whether or not the piano hits her), because she has waived her right against being exposed to the risk. And if Ingrid can *waive* her right against being exposed to what would otherwise be an unreasonable risk of harm, presumably Sandra can *forfeit* her right against being exposed to what would otherwise be an unreasonable risk. If this is correct, then even the lone iteration of the punishment lottery envisioned in the original thought experiment may be impermissible, but this would be neither because it punished Sandra without first establishing her guilt via a fair and reliable process nor even because it subjected Sandra to an unreasonable risk of harm; it would be impermissible instead because it violated the rights of every citizen of Justland other than Sandra not to be exposed to unreasonable risks of harm.

It is worth considering a less far-fetched example, that of an aggressive prosecuting attorney who is happy to break various rules (such as overlooking the fact that evidence was gathered illegally) when he is convinced that the defendant is in fact guilty.[5] At first blush, it might appear that my stance on procedural rights precludes me from condemning this attorney's disregard for the rules, as long as he accurately determines which of the defendants are innocent and which are guilty. After all, if the wrongdoers have forfeited their rights against being punished, and they have no procedural rights, then what does it matter how the evidence was collected? As my analysis of the two variations on my initial thought experiment makes plain, however, there is ample room to criticize this rogue prosecuting attorney. The two obvious points are first, given that we have no reason to believe that prosecuting attorneys are less likely to be fallible than the rest of us, we have compelling reasons to construct criminal legal procedures that institutionally constrain those who occupy these positions. And second, once these laws are duly enacted, prosecuting attorneys are morally bound to respect these rules.

Finally, before concluding this section, it is worth noting that few would deny that an innocent person's rights are violated if she is punished after being duly (and nonculpably) convicted in a fair, reliable, and public trial. But if being duly convicted does not preclude one's rights from being violated, why think that *not* having been duly convicted entails that one's rights *are* necessarily violated? Symmetry suggests that if the presence of a procedurally impeccable determination of guilt cannot ensure that no rights are violated, then the absence of these same procedures would not entail a rights violation. Of course, there is space to adopt an asymmetric stance here, since one can simply assert that punishment necessarily violates rights unless the defendant is both guilty and has been proven to be guilty via an appropriate process. But given that the position I defend here treats the presence and absence of procedural safeguards symmetrically, and because it does not leave us unable to criticize a rogue prosecuting attorney, perhaps critics will be less troubled by my thesis that procedures are justified solely on instrumental grounds.

ASSESSING THE ARGUMENTS IN FAVOR OF PROCEDURAL RIGHTS

The most prominent discussion of judicial procedural rights in the literature is Robert Nozick's landmark analysis in *Anarchy, State, and Utopia*. Nozick focuses on preinstitutional, moral procedural rights because he regards their existence as pivotal to explaining how a group of people might permissibly move from a situation in a state of nature with a dominant protection agency to an ultraminimal state (a situation in which the dominant protective agency comes close to having a de facto monopoly on the use of force within a given territory). Nozick's crucial step boils down to an argument from analogy. He contends that living in a society in which many people personally punish suspects without establishing their guilt via a reliable procedure is analogous to being exposed to a game of Russian roulette; even if one is not wrongly punished, one is exposed to unreasonable risks. And because the clients of the dominant protective agency pay this company to protect them from precisely these types of risks, the agency will legitimately take it upon itself to prohibit "independents" (i.e., those who have not signed up for the agency's services) from punishing any of its clients without first establishing their guilt via a fair and reliable process. What is more, although there is bound to be controversy about whether any given process is fair and/or reliable, the dominant protective agency will be so much more powerful than any of the independents that it alone will have de facto power to unilaterally decide which processes qualify as sufficiently fair and reliable.

Like so much of Nozick's writing, this argument is ingenious. As critics have pointed out, however, it does not work. Most notably, merely establishing that the dominant protective agency's relative power would enable it to coercively impose its own standards of fairness and/or reliability upon the independents does not establish that it is *morally entitled* to do so. And because we seek an explanation of why the state violates no moral rights when it unilaterally asserts itself in this way, Nozick's speculations about the power relations among the various actors is simply beside the point. Even if Nozick could somehow establish that the dominant protective agency could gain the moral right to unilaterally specify which procedures qualify as fair and reliable, though, this would show neither why independents may not permissibly punish clients of the dominant agency as long as they first established the guilt of these clients via the approved procedures, nor why the independents would have to follow these procedures before punishing other independents.

Perhaps Nozick could somehow fortify his arguments so as to rebut these standard objections. We need not explore this possibility here, though, because even if Nozick could successfully buttress his argument against the anarchist, it would not undermine my own claim about the nonexistence of the moral right to a fair trial. The reasons for this can be gleaned from my discussion of the second variation on the initial case involving Sandra. Specifically, while I presumably have a right not to be shot during an unsolicited game of Russian roulette, the wrongdoer has no analogous right against the hard treatment of an appropriate punishment. To put this point in terms of Nozick's example, imagine that, after surviving the piano episode, Ingrid asks me to play Russian roulette with her. Given this request, it seems clear that Ingrid has waived her right against my firing a partially loaded gun at her, and thus whatever risks I expose her to are not unreasonably imposed. And just as Ingrid has waived her rights against being exposed to risks that would otherwise be unreasonable, a wrongdoer might forfeit her right against such risks. So, while those of us who have not acted wrongly may well righteously object to being exposed to the risk of being punished, the wrongdoer has no standing to object to the risk that she might receive a punishment proportionate to her wrongdoing. Thus, whether or not

Nozick's arguments ultimately defeat the anarchist, they clearly do not show that each of us has a moral right not to be punished unless her guilt is first established via a fair and reliable process.[6]

R. A. Duff writes on the morality of our criminal legal institutions with unparalleled insight, subtlety, and sophistication, so it is no surprise that his arguments in defense of the right to a fair trial give me the most pause. Duff surveys several considerations in favor of the conclusion that "we cannot . . . distinguish just ends from just means in the context of a criminal trial."[7] One focuses on our responsibility to avoid mistaken convictions; another utilizes the notion that justice is not done unless it is publicly done; and a third depends upon the defendant's right to be heard. Let us consider each of these in turn.

The first argument Duff considers is essentially that our duty not to punish the innocent combined with our lack of antecedent knowledge about who is guilty requires us to adopt appropriate measures that enable us to reliably distinguish the innocent from the guilty. As Duff puts it:

> If justice requires that we convict only the guilty, every citizen has the right to be convicted only if she is guilty. But we cannot know in advance who is guilty, and we therefore owe it to every citizen to convict her only if we have made reasonably sure that she is guilty; only if we have proved her guilt by reliable procedures which protect the innocent against mistaken conviction. Any citizen accused of an offense thus has the right to be tried in accordance with the requirements of Natural Justice, which specify such reliable procedures, and to be convicted only if her trial has observed these requirements.[8]

Given that innocent folks have not forfeited their rights against being punished, it is hard to deny that we should take great care not to punish those who have done nothing wrong. As Duff ultimately acknowledges, though, this line of reasoning cannot show that any procedural rights exist. The problem is that even if the person who metes out the punishment would be culpable if she did not observe certain procedural safeguards, it does not follow that defendants have a right that these safeguards be followed. One might behave culpably and then—merely because of luck—violate no rights. Imagine, for instance, that Philippa and Elizabeth are in a pub taking turns buying round after round of drinks. And to facilitate payment, each of them has a stack of $20 bills on the table. Suppose that when Elizabeth excuses herself to visit the bathroom, Philippa steals $20 off of Elizabeth's stack and puts it on top of her own stack. And finally, imagine that when Philippa visits the bathroom shortly after Elizabeth's return, Elizabeth takes the top $20 bill from Philippa's stack (the very $20 bill Philippa has just stolen from Elizabeth) and places it on her own pile. Is Elizabeth morally culpable? And if so, has she violated anyone's rights?

My own view is that, while Elizabeth is clearly culpable, she did not violate any rights. Elizabeth is culpable because she *attempted* to steal $20 from Philippa. But because the $20 she tried to steal was (unbeknownst to her) her own money, she merely reclaimed the $20 Philippa had just stolen from her. And since Philippa clearly had no right that Elizabeth not take her money back, Elizabeth (as luck would have it) violated no duties, despite the fact that she is just as culpable as she would have been if she had successfully stolen Philippa's money. If this is correct, it suggests how we should analyze a situation like the initial scenario in which Justland's lottery generated Sandra's name. That is, the Justlanders (or at least the authorities and those who voted in favor of randomly selecting someone to punish) were clearly culpable, because they did not take sufficient care to avoid punishing the innocent. But because the lottery happened to select the person who (unbeknownst to them) did in fact steal the money from the treasury, the Justlanders (as luck would have it) did not violate Sandra's rights. And while I am not sure if Duff conceives of an agent's moral culpability (which I take to be a subjective matter) and the rights she violates (which I take to be an objective matter)[9]) precisely as I do, he ultimately arrives at a similar conclusion when he writes: "But one who is in fact guilty as charged is in no danger of suffering an unjust conviction: if the verdict is in fact correct she suffers neither injustice nor injury. The court acts wrongly, in following an unreliable procedure, but does not wrong *her*."[10]

Duff's second argument is that criminal justice is not done unless it is publicly done. As he explains, "the aim of a criminal trial is not merely to reach an accurate judgment *on* the defendant's past conduct: it is to communicate and justify that judgment—to demonstrate its justice—*to* him and to others. In this context at least, if justice is not both seen and shown to be done, it is not and cannot be done at all."[11] To appreciate the force of Duff's stance, we need look no further than the example of Philippa and Elizabeth. Here Duff might suggest that justice was not fully done when Elizabeth took back her $20 from Philippa precisely because Elizabeth did not publicly take it back for the right reasons. There is a huge difference, Duff might continue, between Elizabeth's publicly demanding $20 from Philippa on the grounds that Philippa must return what she has stolen versus Elizabeth's trying to steal $20 from Philippa (which, unbeknownst to Elizabeth, is actually her own money). And just as Elizabeth's public demand of repayment is preferable to her attempted theft, Justland's punishment of Sandra after determining her guilt via a publicly fair and reliable process is preferable to selecting Sandra by lottery.

In response, I would urge us to distinguish clearly between the *desirability* of these contrasting cases and their *justice*. I certainly agree that it would be preferable, perhaps even morally preferable, that justice should not only be done but publicly done, but I deny that justice is not done unless it is publicly done. I acknowledge that it would be *better* if Elizabeth righteously demanded that Philippa return the

$20 she stole and that the Justlanders publicly establish Sandra's guilt before punishing her, but I am not convinced that Elizabeth necessarily violates anyone's rights when she attempts to steal $20 from Philippa or that Justland violates any rights when it punishes Sandra merely because her name was selected in a random process. To emphasize: I appreciate that justice and publicity are both good things, but they also strike me as distinct things. So while I would obviously prefer justice and publicity to merely justice, I don't see how justice somehow magically turns into injustice in the absence of publicity. Or put in terms of our examples, I do not understand how Philippa's rights are violated merely because no one has publicly offered the appropriate reasons why she may not keep Elizabeth's money, or why Sandra's rights are necessarily violated merely because no one has publicly demonstrated that it is rational to believe that she stole the money from the treasury.[12] And in the absence of a rights violation, I see no grounds for positing the presence of injustice.

A number of prominent scholars have defended the idea that justice is not fully done unless it is publicly done in other contexts, so it is not unreasonable to think that one might try to counter my skepticism about categorizing publicity as an ineliminable component of justice.[13] I will not explore this possibility here, though, because Duff does not place much emphasis on his general claim that "if justice is not both seen and shown to be done, it is not and cannot be done at all." Instead, he focuses on the more specific claim (which I suspect he regards as the crucial instance of his more general contention about publicity) that "both guilty and innocent defendants have a right to be heard which is independent of the right to be acquitted if innocent."[14] This is Duff's strongest and most developed argument on this topic, so it is worth quoting him at length:

> To convict a guilty defendant without giving her a hearing is not to produce a just verdict by unjust means; for the justice

> of a verdict is internally related to the justice of the procedures which produce it. The verdict may express a true judgment on her conduct; but it no longer expresses, as a just verdict must express, the conclusion of a process of rational argument *with* her; she has not been shown that she ought to accept this verdict, since she has not been allowed to participate in the trial. To say that the trial aims to reach an accurate judgment on her conduct, either as a justification for condemning her or as a precondition for punishing her, is therefore at best inadequate and at worst misleading; for it ignores her essential role in her trial as one who is to receive the verdict and participate in the argument which justifies it. The right to be heard is neither simply an instrumental means to some further end, nor simply a side-constraint on our pursuit of consequential goals, but a right which is integral to the meaning and purpose of the criminal trial.[15]

I have a great deal of sympathy for Duff's account, but I regard it as an exceptionally insightful rational reconstruction of what liberal democratic societies currently do (or at least what we aspire to do), rather than an explanation for why we must continue to act as we currently do. I presume that there are weighty instrumental reasons in favor of criminal legal institutions that allow defendants publicly to defend themselves, but I am not convinced that a regime would necessarily violate anyone's rights if it designed the process so that defendants could not be present at the trial. Imagine that we could somehow make trials more likely to convict the guilty, less likely to convict the innocent, and less expensive if we prohibited defendants from entering the courtroom. Suppose that the defendants' presence in the room consistently distracted or otherwise impaired the jurors' ability to clearly and impartially weigh the evidence, for instance. As Malcolm Gladwell suggests:

> We have a jury system in the Western world based on an idea that goes back to antiquity: that the accused has the right to confront his accusers and to be judged by a jury of his peers. Back then it was thought that for justice to be achieved, the jury, the accuser, and the accused all had to see one another. But now we know more: we know that what we see—particularly when it is the color of someone's skin, or gender, or age—does not always aid understanding. Sometimes we can make better judgments with less information. I think that the accused in a criminal trial shouldn't be in the courtroom. He or she should be in another room entirely, answering questions by email or through the use of an intermediary. And I think that all evidence and testimony in a trial that tips the jury off to the age or race or gender of the defendant ought to be edited out.[16]

I am in no position to assert that Gladwell is correct, but what if he is? Would we violate anyone's rights if we changed our institutions accordingly? I think not. Duff might respond that all citizens have a right to be heard that surely is not forfeited when one commits a crime. In his earlier (more Kantian) work, Duff alleges that liberals must conceive of trials (and punishments) as communicative because liberals are committed to respecting every citizen's autonomy. In his later (more communitarian) writing, Duff contends that liberal communities must have trials in order to fulfill their commitment to treating their citizens as responsible members of the normative community. I believe that Duff was wise to abandon his reliance on autonomy, because I do not think that one necessarily violates another's autonomy whenever one fails to publicly provide reasons for one's actions. (I do not believe that Elizabeth violates Philippa's autonomy when she takes the $20 bill off of Philippa's stack without publicly justifying this action, for instance.) As for Duff's more communitarian thesis: If—as I suspect is the case—he merely believes that many liberal communities *do* endorse such a right, then I do not object. But if Duff is insisting that all communities *must* respect this putative right, I am inclined to be skeptical until an argument to that effect is furnished.

Against this dismissal of the right to be heard, Duff might cite our practice of refusing to prosecute, let alone punish, someone who has become insane *after* committing a crime. Imagine, for instance, that Sandra was perfectly healthy when she robbed the treasury, but then lost her sanity before the authorities apprehended her. We would refuse to prosecute and punish Sandra on principled grounds, Duff alleges, because our trials and punishments are essentially about calling upon a fellow citizen to answer for her conduct, and an insane person is patently not capable of answering for her actions. And if I insist that Duff's spiel about publicly answering for crime is merely a description of our current practice rather than a moral prescription that must be followed by all, then I should be prepared to prosecute and punish Insane Sandra, even though she is now unable to answer for her earlier actions. After all, while Sandra's insanity may now render her incapable of forfeiting her rights against being punished, she was perfectly sane when she robbed the treasury, and thus was entirely capable of forfeiting her rights. And if Sandra forfeited her rights when she stole the money, it is hard to see how or why she regained them once she lost her sanity.

There are a number of ways for me to respond to this challenge. Most obviously, I could simply bite the bullet and insist that, while we currently abstain from prosecuting and punishing individuals who have lost their sanity after their wrongdoing, this choice is purely elective. According to this line of thinking, we would no more violate anyone's rights if we were to reverse course and begin punishing folks like Insane Sandra than if we changed a speed limit or altered the time period covered in our criminal statute of limitations. Some may be comfortable with this suggestion, but I must confess that I am not. And given my disapproval of any society that prosecuted those who have lost their sanity after the commission of their crimes, it is incumbent upon me to explain what rights would be violated by this practice.

One possible explanation for the injustice of punishing Insane Sandra is that she has already been punished enough by her loss of sanity.[17] Implicit in this suggestion is the premise that we not only have a right against being punished when we are innocent, we have a right against being overpunished when we are guilty. We do not forfeit all of our rights any time we violate someone else's rights; more modestly (and more plausibly), we forfeit only our right against a "fitting" or proportionate punishment. And if so, then not only can an innocent person's rights be violated when she is punished, a guilty person's rights can be violated when she is overpunished. Finally, if one regards Sandra's loss of sanity as a form of punishment, one might allege that any additional punishment administered by the state would be excessive, and thus would violate Sandra's right against being subjected to a disproportionate punishment.

I have two worries about this very intriguing suggestion. First and most obviously, while I have some sympathy for the notion that the misfortune a criminal has experienced since committing the crime can be a mitigating circumstance that may be taken into consideration when determining an appropriate punishment, I remain uncomfortable with the idea that "the universe" can punish criminals. (In this vein, consider element [iv] of H. L. A. Hart's iconic definition of punishment: "It must be intentionally administered by human beings other than the offender.")[18] More specifically, if Lucky and Unlucky commit a crime together and are not apprehended until five years later, I certainly would deny that Unlucky can assert a moral *right* to a lesser punishment merely because of how much worse her life has gone than Lucky's over the last five years. And second, it is not clear to me that losing one's sanity would always necessarily be at least a proportionate punishment. Imagine an alternate conclusion to World War II, for instance, wherein Hitler fled to Argentina, where he was finally captured, but only after he had lost his sanity. I know of no algorithm with which to determine precisely what punishments fit which crimes, but it does not seem unreasonable to suggest that Hitler acted so monstrously that (while he may not have forfeited his right against any conceivable punishment) even his complete loss of sanity would not be a proportionate punishment. This observation is important because I am more confident that it would be wrong to prosecute and punish Insane Hitler than I am that punishing Insane Hitler would necessarily be an *over*punishment. In light of this, it seems to me that the source of my worries about punishing criminals who have lost their sanity after committing their crimes must be something other than my concern to avoid excessive punishment. And given these two reservations, I would not want to rely on this proposal as my account for why there are principled grounds on which to object to punishing those who have lost their sanity since the commission of their crimes.

My own explanation as to why it is impermissible to punish Insane Sandra for Sane Sandra's crime is that Insane Sandra is not morally responsible for Sane Sandra's actions. Consider, for instance, Victor Tadros's observation that "as the connection between the person as they are now and the person who committed the offence weakens, as it does over time, we have less reason to punish the person, and we are more likely to conclude that punishing her is disproportionate. Imposing severe punishments for offences committed many years ago, even if those offences were very serious, can seem disproportionate. The strength of the connection between the person as she is now and the person as she was when she offended may help to explain this appearance."[19] If Tadros is correct to suggest that the passage of time can undermine the requisite connection between a wrongdoer and her future self (as I believe he is), then it seems unproblematic to suppose that a dramatic psychological shift such as the complete loss of sanity might explain why the now-insane person is not responsible for the crime committed by her earlier, sane self. One way to articulate this idea is in terms of personal identity. On this view, while Insane Sandra is clearly related to (and perhaps a descendant of) Sane Sandra, the former is a distinct person (assuming that she remains a person). Thus, just as it would clearly be impermissible to punish Sandra if (unbeknownst to her) her mother had stolen the money from the state treasury and then bequeathed it to her, it would be unjust to punish Insane Sandra for Sane Sandra's act (even though Sandra/Insane Sandra would not be entitled to keep the money that Sandra's mother/Sane Sandra stole). As Patrick Tomlin has emphasized to me, though, I need not couch this point in such stark (and metaphysically controversial) terms. Even if Sandra remains the same person despite her loss of sanity, there is plenty of room to assert that Insane Sandra is not morally responsible for Sane Sandra's act. As Tomlin expressed in personal correspondence:

> The persistence conditions of personal identity may differ from those of moral responsibility. Given that personal identity with someone who committed an objectively wrongful act is not sufficient for becoming morally responsible (for example, if they were sleepwalking), it is not clear why personal identity would be sufficient for retaining moral responsibility. If we look at the kinds of theories compatibilists in particular advance for one's becoming responsible (such as "real self" or "intellectual process" views), then these would seem to suggest particular persistence conditions (an act's still being the product of one's "real self," or one's still having the right connection to the "intellectual process").

In the end, then, I agree with Duff that there are principled reasons not to prosecute or punish those who have become insane after their wrongdoing, but I deny that this vindicates the preinstitutional right to be heard. I continue to value Duff's account of trials and punishments as an insightful rational reconstruction of what liberal democratic regimes currently (aspire to) do, but I do not think there is a general moral right to be heard that requires all societies to design their judicial systems to utilize inclusive, fair, and reliable processes for publicly determining the guilt of each defendant. And I do not regard the requirement that we refrain from prosecuting and punishing defendants who have lost their sanity after committing their crimes as a glaring counterexample to my position, because I believe this prohibition is better explained by the impermissibility of punishing people for acts for which they are not morally responsible.

THE HUMAN RIGHT TO DUE PROCESS

Article 10 of the Universal Declaration of Human Rights states: "Everyone is entitled in full equality to a fair and public hearing by an independent and impartial tribunal, in the determination of his rights and obligations and of any criminal charge against him." People routinely mock the putative human right to paid holidays, many question the human right to healthcare, and since the publication of Rawls's *Law of Peoples* it has become fashionable to wonder aloud about the human right to democracy, but *no one* doubts that there is a human right to due process. So the fact that my position seems to imply that we must dramatically revise the core international human rights documents will strike many as a decisive objection. The reasoning behind this criticism is straightforward: Human rights are often conceived of as being a subset of individual moral rights, which are distinguished in terms of their connection to basic human interests, and they are also typically understood to be particularly urgent moral rights that must be respected by all legitimate states. But if I deny that there are moral rights to due process, clearly my view is incompatible with the existence of universal and especially weighty moral rights to due process. And given that I have explicitly argued that states are at liberty to play fast and loose with their criminal legal procedures if doing so would enable them to maximize various institutional goals, I certainly cannot allege that due process rights are morally sacrosanct commitments from which no country may permissibly deviate.

This line of critique is tempting, but it should be resisted because of its failure to distinguish between moral and legal human rights. I think the best way to read the core human rights documents like the Universal Declaration of Human Rights is as statements of international law. In other words, the Universal Declaration of Human Rights undeniably purports to list human rights, but these are best understood as international *legal* rights. Of course, those inclined to press this critique against my view might concede that human rights documents are designed to create international legal human rights but insist that these documents champion the particular rights they do only because of a belief in corresponding (and preexisting) moral rights. In other words, documents like the Universal Declaration of Human Rights are designed to create legal rights that faithfully capture our convictions regarding moral human rights.

I do not doubt that many conceive of the Universal Declaration of Human Rights in these terms, but the most sophisticated theorists in this area certainly reject this approach. In *The Heart of Human Rights*, for instance, Allen Buchanan emphatically rejects the idea (which he calls "the mirroring view") that "to justify an international legal human right typically involves defending the claim that a corresponding moral human right exists."[20] Against the mirroring view, Buchanan advocates a "pluralistic justificatory methodology" that "allows for the possibility that in some cases, perhaps many cases international legal human rights can be justified without appealing to corresponding, preexisting moral rights, but instead by appealing to other moral considerations."[21] To see the logic behind this approach, notice that domestic lawmakers routinely create legal rights that do not correspond to antecedent moral rights and make laws that fail to legally protect antecedent moral rights. Consider how such lawmakers might deliberate about whether to legalize physician-assisted suicide, for instance. Legislators should no doubt consider whether physicians have a moral right to assist in suicides, but this is certainly not the only relevant consideration. Lawmakers might have compelling reasons to create a legal right to physician-assisted suicide even if there is no antecedent moral right, and they may have sufficient reason to criminalize this practice even if physicians have a moral right to engage in it. And if we recognize that legal rights need not strictly correspond to preexisting moral rights in the domestic realm, it should be clear that the two need not mirror one another in the international legal arena either.

With this in mind, it is worth retracing James Nickel's defense of human rights to due process. In general, Nickel proposes six steps to justifying a specific human right:

> The first step requires showing that people today regularly experience problems or abuses in the area protected by the proposed right. The second step is to show that this norm has the importance or high priority that is a key feature of human rights. We do this by showing the right protects things that are central to a decent life as a person. . . . The third step in justifying a specific human right involves seeing if the proposed norm . . . can . . . be formulated as a right of all people that they have independently of recognition or enactment at the national level. . . . The fourth test requires showing that a norm as strong as a right is needed to provide this protection, that no weaker measures will

> be sufficiently effective. The fifth criterion is that the burdens the right imposes are neither excessive nor severely unfair. The sixth and final test requires that human rights be feasible to implement in an ample majority of countries today.[22]

For my purposes, I can focus on the first two steps, which (as Nickel acknowledges) follow from Henry Shue's recommendation that human rights should be thought of as "a rationally justified demand for social guarantees against standard threats."[23] Putting all of this together, one concludes that, while the framers of international legal documents like the Universal Declaration of Human Rights need not ignore questions about antecedent moral rights, their primary focus should be on the standard threats to living a minimally decent life in modern society.

Having adopted this approach, Nickel is well positioned to furnish a strong defense of international legal human rights to due process, given his observation that "tyrants throughout history have used the institutions, personnel, and sanctions of the criminal law as means of imposing their arbitrary and unjust rule. They throw their enemies and political opponents into jail, have them executed, or take away their property. The authors of historic and contemporary bills of rights were well aware of these dangers and accordingly gave due process rights a prominent place."[24] In short, we can offer a compelling case for creating international legal human rights to due process in view of the obvious fact that one of the standard threats to living a decent life has historically been the abuses perpetrated by those who control the criminal legal institutions.

Nickel's analysis is particularly instructive, in part because he is one of the most sophisticated human rights theorists, but also because he believes in moral rights to due process and therefore has no stake in my thesis that there are no general, moral, judicial procedural rights. Thus, not only do I take solace in the fact that nothing about my position precludes me from affirming Nickel's defense of international legal human rights to due process, I am especially heartened that a leading human rights theorist would pursue this particular approach *even though he could have focused exclusively on moral rights to due process instead*. We can thus safely conclude that, while my position certainly denies the existence of an entire category of moral rights that most of us are pretheoretically inclined to accept, it does not place me at odds with the best understanding of core international legal documents like the Universal Declaration of Human Rights.

CONCLUSION

Few believe that there is a preinstitutional moral right to drive a certain speed along a given stretch of highway, and not many of us would claim that jurisdictions are morally barred from altering their statutes of limitations so as to extend the amount of time before citizens become legally immune to criminal prosecution for earlier crimes. Some judicial procedural rights, however, are typically regarded as nonnegotiable. If any country refused to treat its subjects as innocent until proven guilty, if it prosecuted citizens multiple times for the same crime, or if it punished suspected criminals without first duly establishing their guilt via a fair, reliable, and public trial, for instance, then critics would denounce the offending regime for egregiously violating the basic moral rights of its constituents. If my arguments in this chapter have been on target, however, such a critique would be misguided. Governments clearly have pressing reasons to carefully design their criminal legal institutions so that none of their citizens is vulnerable to being wrongly punished, overpunished, or otherwise harassed by government officials, but their reasons for doing so do not derive from antecedent moral procedural rights. Absent special circumstances, there are no preinstitutional procedural rights, not even a right against being punished without first being found guilty by a fair, reliable, and public process.

Chapter 6

The Problem of Relatedness

As I explained during my discussion of procedural rights, I believe that an agent's reasons for acting do not determine the deontic status of her action. Adopting objectivism with respect to moral obligation apparently spells trouble for the rights forfeiture theory of punishment, however, because it suggests that those who have forfeited their rights may permissibly be punished for any reason whatsoever. Warren Quinn first pointed this out in his seminal essay "The Right to Threaten and the Right to Punish." He writes:

> The proper authorities are entitled to punish Jones, a generally decent young man who has foolishly stolen Smith's car, by depriving him of up to the amount of liberty forfeited in the theft. But suppose that before any such punishment takes place, Smith, for reasons having nothing whatever to do with the theft, kidnaps Jones and deprives him of exactly that amount of liberty. In this situation it is natural to suppose that Smith not only wrongs Jones but specifically violates his right to liberty. Perhaps this is because Jones forfeits his right to the community as a whole and not to Smith in particular. But suppose that the community in which Jones lives has the unjust practice of seizing and confining political dissenters. And suppose that shortly after his crime Jones, who also happens to be a dissenter, is officially seized

> and, for a time, quarantined to prevent the spread of his political views (views having nothing to do with his theft). Again, we would naturally suppose that Jones's right to liberty had been violated by his community, even if he were confined only for a period that would constitute an acceptable punishment for his theft and were never punished thereafter.[1]

Quinn's worry (which Richard Lippke has since labeled "the problem of relatedness") interrogates forfeiture theory's pivotal claim that it is permissible to punish Jones because, in stealing Smith's car, Jones forfeited his right against imprisonment.[2] The concern, of course, is that if Jones has forfeited his right against hard treatment, he has no right against Smith randomly kidnapping him (as long as the conditions and duration of this kidnapping do not exceed what would constitute a proportionate prison sentence). But surely Smith would violate Jones's right if Smith kidnapped Jones, even if Jones (unbeknownst to Smith) had stolen Smith's car.

To appreciate how awkward the implications could be, recall that I have already argued for a competitive right to punish and against the existence of judicial procedural rights. Thus, at least in the state of nature, anyone would be at liberty to impose the hard treatment, and one could not object to Smith's kidnapping Jones on the grounds that Smith is harming Jones without first establishing his guilt via a fair and reliable process. Unless we specify that wrongdoers may permissibly be harmed only for reasons appropriately related to their wrongdoing, then we may not object to even the worst types of wanton violence. As John Simmons notes, "If the criminal simply forfeits his right not to be harmed in certain ways, then *any* way in which this harm is imposed appears morally acceptable, *any* reason a person has for imposing it is good enough. If Butch and his gang roam the state of nature, cutting throats at random, just for the fun of it, and happen to cut the throat of a murderer (who deserves to be punished with a painful death, say), then that particular throat-cutting, but no other, might be morally acceptable. This seems a preposterous implication."[3] In other words, if Butch and his gang randomly kill a murderer and four others in the state of nature, then unless the forfeiture theorist can somehow establish that a wrongdoer has forfeited her right only to be harmed *for reasons related to her wrongdoing*, this view has the awkward implication that Butch and his cohort have actually committed only four, rather than five, impermissible acts.

An obvious way to avoid these unpalatable implications is simply to *stipulate* that the forfeiture theory of punishment must be understood as the view that wrongdoers forfeit their rights only against being harmed for certain reasons (i.e., reasons appropriately related to the wrongdoing). Jeff McMahan makes this type of move when he explains and defends his forfeiture theory of killing in war. He writes: "It is sometimes objected to theories of forfeiture that if, for example, a person forfeits his right to life, that must mean that anyone may permissibly kill him, for any reason, at any time. But the form of forfeiture that corresponds to liability to attack in war is highly specific. For a person to cease to be innocent in war, all that is necessary is the forfeiture of the right not to be attacked *for certain reasons*, by certain persons, in certain conditions."[4] Following McMahan's lead, then, a proponent of the forfeiture theory of punishment can easily sidestep this objection by distinguishing between what Stephen Kershnar has labeled "limited-reasons" and "unlimited-reasons" accounts, and then insisting that she means to defend only the former.[5] The core idea here is straightforward: If the unlimited-reasons account (i.e., the view that a wrongdoer forfeits her right against being subjected to hard treatment for any reason whatsoever) leads to unacceptable conclusions, this shows only that we should advance the limited-reasons approach (the view that wrongdoers forfeit their right against being harmed only for reasons appropriately related to their wrongdoing); it gives us no reason to jettison forfeiture theory as a whole.

For two reasons, I am not entirely satisfied with this response. First, critics might object that it is ad hoc to merely stipulate that we should eschew the unlimited-reasons approach; at the very least, it would be preferable if we could provide some type of argument that explains why forfeiture theory should be construed in a limited-reasons fashion. Second, I doubt that liability to attack in war is in fact limited in the fashion McMahan suggests.

To see why I disagree with McMahan on this point, imagine that Emma, Lola, and Zoe are three women living in France in 1942. First consider Emma. Emma has a gentle disposition and is terribly distraught about the holocaust. After many sleepless nights spent agonizing over the atrocities, Emma finally decides to assassinate Adolf Hitler. Emma abhors the thought of killing another human being, but she has become convinced that Hitler has forfeited his right to life because of his moral responsibility for the unjust threat he poses to European Jews (among others). She therefore summons the courage and ultimately kills Hitler.

Next imagine that Lola hates Germans so much that she would like nothing better than to kill one. And while Lola expects that she would enjoy killing any German, she would like to kill the most prominent German possible. Because of this, she often lies awake at night fantasizing about assassinating Hitler. Lola does not want to act unjustly, though, so she resolves never to act on her anti-German animus. One night, however, it dawns on Lola that Hitler has made himself morally liable to assassination because of his responsibility for the unjust threat he poses to European Jews (among others). Lola has no strong feelings about the holocaust (and she certainly would not risk her life on behalf of the many victims of the Third Reich), but she now recognizes that she may permissibly indulge her chauvinistic desires by killing Hitler. She thus takes advantage of the "moral cover" that Hitler has provided her by forfeiting his right to life, and she assassinates him.

Finally, consider Zoe, who is like Lola in that she routinely fantasizes about killing Germans, and she particularly relishes the idea of assassinating Hitler. Unlike Lola, however, Zoe is not troubled by the thought that she might act impermissibly; only her fear of being punished has deterred her from killing a German. Ultimately, though, Zoe decides that the thrill of killing Hitler is worth the considerable personal risk. It never dawns on her that killing Hitler may be permissible (indeed, Zoe has never given the holocaust much thought); she thus moves forward with her plan despite being convinced that she will be violating Hitler's right to life. Zoe assassinates Hitler.

Have Emma, Lola, and/or Zoe all acted permissibly, or has any of them violated Hitler's right to life? I appreciate that the targeted killing of another human being is a ghastly act, so I can understand why a pacifist might insist that none of these women has acted permissibly. For the purposes of this discussion, though, I shall assume without argument that assassination can be morally permissible in extreme instances, and that Hitler in 1942 constitutes just such a case.[6] More specifically, let us follow McMahan in saying that those who are morally responsible for an unjust threat can forfeit their rights, and thus I begin by presuming that Emma has acted permissibly. (Indeed, I would not hesitate to go further and say that Emma behaved in an exemplary fashion and revealed herself to have an admirable character.) I recognize that not everyone will agree with this assessment, but I shall not dwell further on Emma, because Lola and Zoe are the more relevant cases.

What should we say of Lola? What do we think of her character, and has she acted impermissibly? Lola's character seems mixed. On the one hand, she is to be applauded for her steadfast refusal to violate the rights of others. On the other hand, her violent anti-German bias seems utterly despicable. As vile as this component of her character may be, though, it does not follow that she has necessarily acted unjustly. On the contrary, given that Hitler has forfeited his right to life, it seems clear that neither he nor anyone else has any grounds to object to the fact that Lola killed him. It is certainly unsettling to know how much joy Lola took in this gruesome act, but, again, this shows only that there are regrettable elements of Lola's character, not that she acted impermissibly.

What about Zoe? Her character seems thoroughly contemptible. Not only does she share Lola's deplorable anti-German animus, Zoe is utterly unmoved by the moral rights of others. And because she happily killed Hitler even though she believed that she was inexcusably violating his right to life, she is culpable in a way that Lola is not. Despite all of this, I deny that Zoe has acted impermissibly. In my view, Zoe is no less culpable than she would be if she had violated Hitler's right to life, but she did not in fact wrong Hitler, because he forfeited his right to life and thus had no claim against Zoe that she not kill him. Against this moral analysis, McMahan might object that Zoe did wrong Hitler, because Hitler did not forfeit his right against being killed for unlimited reasons; more minimally, he forfeited his right only against being killed for defensive reasons. And because it never even occurred to Zoe that Hitler might have been permissibly assassinated in defense of others, she clearly did not kill for the right reasons. As a consequence, McMahan might say that, unlike Emma (and perhaps Lola), Zoe acted impermissibly because she violated Hitler's right to life.[7]

How can we adjudicate between those who allege that Zoe's act was impermissible and those who contend that it was suberogatory? Is this simply a matter over which reasonable people can disagree? One potential way to help settle the dispute is to consider our convictions about the rights of third parties to interfere. In my view, all rights may be (proportionately) coercively enforced, so if Hitler had a right that Emma, Lola, and/or Zoe not kill him (or if anyone else had a right that Hitler not be killed), a third party would be morally permitted to interfere with these women when they attempted to assassinate Hitler. If it was morally permissible for any of these three to assassinate Hitler, however, then others would have a duty not to forcibly interfere with her attempt to do so. This line of thought is confirmed by the fact (assuming that it is a fact) that most agree that it would be impermissible for a third party to interfere with Emma's or Lola's plans to kill Hitler. But what should we say about a third party resisting Zoe? In my view, one would not be justified in preventing Zoe from carrying out her plan. As acknowledged earlier, Zoe's motivation and character are thoroughly reprehensible, but this observation seems the wrong type of consideration to justify a third party's forcibly interfering with Zoe's assassination. After all, what could someone inclined to forcibly resist Zoe's assassination attempt say to her—"It is true that Hitler's moral responsibility for the massive unjust threat posed by the Nazi regime entails that he has forfeited his right against lethal defensive force, but I am nonetheless going to block your efforts to kill Hitler, because it has never occurred to you that Hitler has forfeited his life"? And if I am correct that no third party may permissibly thwart Zoe's actions, this supports my contention that Zoe's actions are not contrary to duty.

It is worth noting that this type of reasoning is not specific to rights forfeiture; I think we should analyze rights that are overridden or waived in similar fashion. For a case in which rights are overridden, we can borrow an example from Frances Kamm. In *Ethics for Enemies,* Kamm asks us to imagine that the United States is occupied by a Nazi regime that houses its military operations in the World Trade Center. She supposes that members of the Resistance would be morally permitted to bomb the World Trade Center (which contains no civilians) even if doing so would unavoidably kill nonresponsible civilians who live nearby. Assuming that the number of civilians killed is not disproportionate, I believe that Kamm is right to regard this act as morally justified. And because the civilians have neither waived nor forfeited their rights against being harmed, this lethal act of resistance would be permissible only if the civilians' rights were overridden. Thus, while it would normally violate the rights of nonresponsible civilians if one detonated a bomb in their vicinity, this act is permissible in these extraordinary circumstances only because it is necessary to defeat the Nazi regime occupying the United States.

Things quickly become more interesting, however, when Kamm imagines a group that she calls the "Baby Killer Nation." As she explains, Baby Killer Nation is "interested in destroying the Nazi's military operations in the WTC only because this is a means to satisfy its own bad desire to cause harm and terror to babies and children living nearby. They have this as an end, but also as a means to protest Nazi pronatalism. Baby Killer Nation members act on their desire to kill babies only when there is an act in a just cause (such as destroying a Nazi state) that can act 'as a pretext.'"[8] Kamm specifies that all members of Baby Killer Nation are afraid of being punished, and thus they carry out only those missions that would be permissible if done by members of the Resistance.

Going beyond Kamm's example, we can imagine a third group, the *Brazen* Baby Killer Nation. Like Baby Killer Nation, Brazen Baby Killer Nation wants to kill babies and young children. Unlike those in Baby Killer Nation, though, the members of Brazen Baby Killer Nation are unfazed by the prospects of punishment, and thus do not limit themselves to permissible acts of violence. And finally, imagine that the Brazen Baby Killer Nation bombs the World Trade Center without any awareness that doing so is a permissible act of resistance against the Nazi regime; they do so simply because it strikes them as a good way to cause harm and terror to babies and children in the vicinity.

Do members of the Baby Killer Nation and Brazen Baby Killer Nation act permissibly when they bomb the World Trade Center?

I believe that they do. There is undeniably something problematic about the character of the members of Baby Killer Nation (and the members of Brazen Baby Killer Nation are considerably more deplorable), but as I have shown above, it does not follow from this that either of them acts impermissibly. In defense of this judgment, consider whether it would be permissible for a third party to forcibly interfere with the missions of either the Baby Killer Nation or the Brazen Baby Killer Nation. If either Nation was violating the moral rights of the Nazi soldiers within the World Trade Center or the civilians in the vicinity, then third parties would be justified in using proportionate force to protect these victims. But because the Nazi officials have forfeited their rights against proportionate defensive force, and because the rights of the civilians in the area have been overridden in this case, a third party is no more justified in resisting members of Baby Killer Nation or Brazen Baby Killer Nation than she would be were she to interfere with the Resistance. And if third parties may not permissibly interfere, this lends support to my conclusion that (however deplorable their characters may be) the members of neither Nation act impermissibly when bombing the World Trade Center.

Finally, consider rights that have been waived. In particular, imagine that the city of St. Louis initiates a program of donating cars, wherein those who wish to give their old cars to others can simply leave them (with their keys in the ignition) on a specially designated donation lot, where anyone who wants a used car is perfectly free to take it. Imagine that Smith wins the lottery and then decides to abandon her relatively new Range Rover on this donation lot. Johnson happens to be walking by the lot at the time. She is stunned to see someone donating such a new and expensive car, so she runs to Smith's (former) car and drives off, giddy with pleasure at her good fortune. Given that Smith has waived her right to her car, it seems clear that Johnson has acted permissibly.

But now consider McCoy, who also happens to be walking by when she sees Smith leave her keys in the ignition of her Range Rover. McCoy has come to St. Louis specifically to steal a car and knows nothing about the donation lot. Finally, suppose that McCoy sneaks over to Smith's (former) car and then drives off, giddy with pleasure at her good fortune. Given that McCoy believes that she is stealing Smith's car, she seems just as culpable as someone who is actually stealing a luxury car. Because one can act culpably without acting impermissibly, though, we cannot infer anything about the permissibility of McCoy's act from her culpability. And in my view, even though McCoy is just as culpable as a car thief, she is (merely as a matter of luck) not actually stealing a car. Because Smith has (unbeknownst to McCoy) abandoned her car, McCoy is in fact rightfully taking possession of an unowned object, just as if she were picking up an apple that had fallen from an unowned apple tree. Finally, notice that third parties would be prohibited from forcibly interfering with McCoy's taking possession of the Range Rover (just as they would be prohibited from interfering with McCoy's picking an unowned apple up off the ground), and this once again confirms the conclusion that (despite her culpability) McCoy acts permissibly when she takes possession of Smith's (former) car.

At this point, it might be helpful to pull back from these various thought experiments to take stock of where we stand in the larger dialectic. We began with the problem of relatedness, the concern that the forfeiture theory of punishment implies that people might permissibly harm wrongdoers for reasons totally unrelated to their wrongdoing. In response, we considered following McMahan's lead and endorsing a limited-reasons rights forfeiture view, which stipulates that a wrongdoer forfeits her right only against proportionate hard treatment that is imposed *in response* to the wrongdoing. The cases I have presented, though, indicate that we do not typically think that an agent may permissibly act only for certain reasons when a right is overridden, waived, or forfeited in other contexts, so perhaps it would not be so "preposterous" (as Simmons puts it) if the rights forfeiture theory of punishment entailed that wrongdoers may permissibly be harmed for reasons unrelated to their wrongdoing. As I acknowledged in chapter 5, there have certainly been some prominent advocates of subjective accounts of duties, but most theorists cash out culpability in subjective terms and conceive of obligation in objective terms. Putting this in terms of Simmons's example of Butch (who randomly slits the throat of a person in the state of nature who—unbeknownst to Butch—forfeited his right against capital punishment), perhaps we should say that, even though Butch is every bit as culpable as a murderer, he actually acted permissibly in this case. I appreciate that many will continue to resist this conclusion, but our analysis of cases in which rights are overridden, waived, or forfeited in other contexts indicates that the "*problem* of relatedness" should be reconceived as the "*question* of relatedness." That is, given that theorists often believe that an agent's reasons for acting do not determine the deontic status of her act, we should not automatically regard it as a reductio if a theory of punishment implies this as well. And finally, if there is some reason that Butch acts impermissibly, it may well be specific to punishment. To emphasize: there may be something distinctive about punishment that explains why those who mete out the hard treatment must do so for reasons related to wrongdoing, but unless we can furnish some type of argument to this effect, singling out punishment as limited-reasons seems ad hoc.

SIMMONS ON LIMITED-REASONS

The most thorough and sophisticated defense of the limited-reasons approach by a rights forfeiture theorist remains John Simmons's discussion in "Locke and the Right to Punish." Simmons offers four distinct arguments for the limited-reasons approach, so let us consider each in turn.

To begin, Simmons indicates that he favors limited-reasons more globally, and thus his comments about punishment are not merely a move designed to save only the forfeiture theory of punishment. He makes this clear when he writes: "If I take property from someone who, completely unbeknownst to me, had previously stolen *my* property, my taking is still theft (and morally impermissible)—even though the property I took from him I might have been entitled to take, if I had taken it *as reparation*. Similarly, the throat-cutting Butch imposes is murder, not justifiable punishment, though he might have been entitled to kill if he had done so *as punishment*."[9]

As should be clear from my examples above, I simply disagree with Simmons's analysis of theft and reparations. To appreciate my view on this point, imagine that Sue and Russ both own silver Toyota Priuses, and each learns via an email from Toyota that there is a defect with their keys that may enable them to work on other people's Priuses. On a whim, Sue tries her key on Russ's Prius, and when she finds that it works, she steals Russ's car and drives it to a party. As luck would have it, Russ is also at this party, and on a similar whim, he tries his key on a car he thinks is Sue's. And when Russ finds that his key works on (the car he mistakes for) Sue's car, he decides to steal this car rather than walk home. According to Simmons, Sue and Russ both impermissibly steal cars. I would analyze the situation differently. I concede that Russ is just as culpable as Sue, but I contend that Russ has neither stolen anything nor acted impermissibly. Russ admittedly *attempted* to steal Sue's car, but because the vehicle was (unbeknownst to Russ) actually his own car, Russ merely (inadvertently) reclaimed his own possession. And to confirm my interpretation over Simmons's, think about what rights we believe Sue and third parties would have against Russ. In particular, notice that, even though it seems appropriate to condemn Russ for what he believes he is doing, neither Sue nor any third party appears entitled to forcibly interfere with Russ's efforts to drive (what is in fact his own car) home. If Russ were really stealing a car as Simmons alleges, then Sue and others would be entitled to use proportionate force to thwart this impermissible act. But what does Simmons imagine Sue might say to Russ on such an occasion—"This is in fact your car, but it is impermissible for you to drive it home because, for all you know, it is indeed mine!"?

Simmons's second argument is that if one can *waive* one's right against certain acts for limited reasons, then there is nothing mysterious about the idea that one might forfeit one's rights against hard treatment that is imposed only for limited reasons. As Simmons puts it, "we often *voluntarily* transfer to others rights to act only for certain reasons (e.g., you may give your doctor the right to act during your upcoming surgery as he thinks best—but only when he acts for medical reasons, as opposed, say, to acting for financial reasons or to enhance his professional reputation). If we may voluntarily create a situation where others have rights to act only for certain reasons, it seems plausible to suppose that nonvoluntary forfeiture might result, as I have claimed that it must, in rights to harm another for only certain reasons."[10]

As one might infer from my example of the Range Rover that Smith abandons on the donation lot, my view on waived rights is different. Someone who abandons property waives a right *in rem* whereas a patient who consents to a doctor's performing a specific surgery waives a right *in personam*, but this distinction has no bearing on whether the agent's reasons for acting can affect the deontic status of her act. Doctors have a moral responsibility to counsel us honestly about our health, and thus it would obviously be impermissible for a surgeon to mislead me about the potential benefits of a given procedure just so that she could make some money. Imagine, though, that, based upon my doctor's advice, I consent to her removing one of my kidneys in one month's time. My physician (who has a gambling problem) loses more than she can spare in an illegal poker game the night before my scheduled surgery, and the person to whom she has lost tells her that he will forgive all of the debt if my physician brings him a kidney within twenty-four hours. My doctor is desperate, so she sneaks into the hospital with the intent to steal a kidney. And as luck would have it, there I am, left alone in an operating room. My physician does not recognize me (or remember that she was scheduled to remove my kidney); she regards me as some random, unattended victim from whom she can steal a kidney. Thus, she removes my kidney and then sneaks off with it to pay her gambling debt. Has she stolen my kidney, or has she (unbeknownst to her) merely completed the medical procedure she had agreed to perform? In my view, the physician is just as culpable as she would be if she had stolen a kidney, but she merely unwittingly performed a routine (and permissible) surgery. I thus disagree with Simmons's assessment that we can waive our rights that others act only for certain types of reasons.

Simmons next alleges that fairness weighs in favor of the limited-reasons account. He writes:

> The unfairness to others that would be involved in allowing the criminal to *retain* his full complement of rights is unfairness only to those who themselves *obey* the relevant rules. Butch, with others who harm for the *wrong* reasons, is *not* obeying the rules in the relevant sense—that is, he is not prepared to deliberately limit his own liberty according to his view of what is required by fair rules. Indeed, he demonstrates his unwillingness to obey the rules in the very act of attempting to inflict the harm, since he *believes* the act *not* to be one of just punishment. There is thus no obvious unfairness to Butch in allowing a criminal to retain his right not to be harmed for Butch's reasons. Fairness (thus

> forfeiture) is at issue only in relation to those who *do* obey the rules and attempt to harm others only for acceptable reasons.[11]

While I am not inclined to ground rights forfeiture in the value of fairness, it is hard to contest the moral importance of fairness, and it would certainly be preferable if one's favored account of forfeiture was not patently unfair. With this in mind, we should think carefully about Butch and the moral consequences of his actions. In particular, one might worry about my pronouncement that Butch acts permissibly when he randomly slits the throat of someone who (unbeknownst to Butch) has forfeited her right against capital punishment, because Butch is no less culpable than Barb (who, let us imagine, randomly slits the throat of an innocent person), and Barb thereby forfeits her right against punishment. But given that Butch and Barb are equally culpable and mere luck explains why Butch acted permissibly, why should only Barb be morally liable to punishment?

I agree that it is problematic to say that Barb becomes morally liable to punishment whereas Butch remains morally immune, but a forfeiture theory of punishment need not imply this. A forfeiture theorist can hold that Butch is also liable to punishment because, even though it turned out that his victim had forfeited her right against being killed, Butch *thought* he was murdering an innocent victim. In my view, for instance, rights-related culpability is necessary and sufficient to make oneself morally liable to punishment.[12] Admittedly, this theory of criminal attempts entails that one can forfeit a right without violating a right (since Butch would be culpable—and thus would have forfeited his right—even though he had not violated anyone else's right), but in the absence of a compelling reason to insist that only rights violators forfeit rights, this should not lead us to eschew an account of criminal attempts that both accords with fairness and comes recommended by leading theorists of criminal law on other grounds.[13]

Simmons's final argument in favor of the limited-reasons approach is that those who harm wrongdoers for reasons unrelated to their wrongdoing disrespect the wrongdoer. As he puts it:

> Harming others (who deserve punishment) for the wrong reasons is morally wrong in the same way that disproportionate punishment of wrongdoers is wrong. Both fail to *respond* to the person and what he did, both fail to respect him and take him seriously. . . . Since the possession of rights is premised on autonomy and moral agency, forfeiture of rights is similarly restricted—we forfeit rights by our misconduct only to the extent that makes possible *respectful* punishment. . . . The same style of argument that Locke could use to justify his insistence on proportionality of punishment (II, 8), then, can be used to justify this limit on the *reasons* for which we may legitimately harm wrongdoers.[14]

I agree with Simmons both that (1) wrongdoers forfeit their rights only against a proportionate punishment, and (2) those who over-punish wrongdoers wrongfully disrespect their victims. I also think that Butch culpably disrespects the person whose throat he cuts even though (unbeknownst to Butch) she lacks a right against having her throat cut. It is important to bear in mind, though, the difference between *culpably* disrespecting someone and *wrongly* disrespecting her. Normally, those who culpably disrespect someone also wrongly disrespect that person, but it is possible to culpably disrespect someone without wrongly disrespecting her, and it is possible to wrongly disrespect someone without culpably disrespecting her. For an example of the latter, imagine that authorities in a legitimate state punish an innocent person after she has been duly (but mistakenly) convicted of stealing a car. What is more, imagine that (perhaps because the defendant was cleverly framed) all of the police, prosecutors, and jury members acted faultlessly during the entire process leading up to the erroneous conviction. Because the duly convicted person is in fact innocent, the authorities wrongly disrespect her when they mete out their punishment. But because the authorities have acted precisely as they should have given the evidence available to them, they do not culpably disrespect this wrongly convicted person.

With this in mind, think again of Butch. Insofar as he has no reason to believe that the random person whose throat he slashes deserves to be capitally punished, Butch unquestionably culpably disrespects her when he ruthlessly kills her. Because she has forfeited her right against capital punishment, however, it turns out that Butch does not *wrongly* disrespect her. Thus, if we assume that a typical overpunisher both wrongly and culpably disrespects those she overpunishes, then Simmons would be correct to say that Butch is like the overpunisher in *culpably* disrespecting the murderer. Unlike the overpunisher, however, Butch does not *wrongly* disrespect the murderer, because the latter is not in fact owed (this type of) respect. If this is correct, we may concede that Butch's culpability resembles a typical person who either punishes an innocent victim or overpunishes a guilty person but nevertheless resist Simmons's conclusion that Butch has necessarily acted impermissibly. In the end, then, I am not sure that any of Simmons's four arguments in defense of the limited-reasons approach will suffice.

TOWARD A NEW ACCOUNT

Although I am not entirely satisfied with Simmons's arguments (and despite my general sympathy for objectivism regarding obligation), I remain uncomfortable with the idea that Butch has acted permissibly. To pinpoint my discomfort, consider again the example in which Sue takes advantage of the defective car keys, steals Russ's Prius, and drives it to a party that Russ also attends. For the sake of argument, let us assume that there is nothing in principle objectionable about corporal punishment, and that a fitting punishment for stealing a car of this value is ten lashes with a one-inch-wide leather belt.[15] As I mentioned above, I believe that Russ would act culpably but permissibly if, when leaving the party, he attempted to steal what he mistook as Sue's (but was actually his own) Prius and drove it home. And in support of this conclusion, I noted that it seems awkward to suppose that anyone might permissibly interfere with Russ's actions (which in fact amount only to reclaiming his own car).[16] But now consider a variation on this example: suppose that Russ is a horribly violent drunk and that he drinks too much at this party and then decides to find a hapless victim to beat up. Imagine that he says to himself: "This party is boring, I am going to go out and beat the first person I come across like he stole my car." Russ thus leaves the party and, coincidentally, the first person he sees on the street is Sue, who (unbeknownst to Russ) has just stolen his car and driven it to the party. Finally, imagine that Russ wrestles Sue to the ground and whips her ten times with his one-inch-wide belt. Has Russ acted permissibly?

Despite my attraction to objectivism regarding obligation, I am reluctant to say so. (And consistent with this, I am tempted to say not only that bystanders might be excused in protecting Sue from Russ's beating, but that they would be permitted to interfere.) But why? If the fact that Sue has no moral claim to Russ's car explains why Russ acts permissibly in taking the car (even when he believes he is stealing an innocent victim's car), why does the fact that Sue has forfeited her right against ten lashes not also explain why Russ acts permissibly in meting out this hard treatment (even though he believes he is merely beating up an innocent victim)? What the comparison of these two cases reveals, I think, is that if Russ's beating is really impermissible, it is not because we should generally embrace subjectivism regarding obligation; as I indicated above, it is because there is something distinctive about punishment that requires that those who mete out the punishment must do so for the right reasons.

The best way to capture what is distinctive about punishment might be to redirect our attention to what rights the punished person can claim. Consider the following five distinct cases. And for the sake of argument, let us suppose that a proportionate punishment for stealing a $30,000 car or boat would be a six-month prison sentence. That is, let us assume that someone who steals a car or boat of this value forfeits her rights against being incarcerated for up to six months. If a car or boat thief were imprisoned for longer than six months, however, that would violate her rights.

First, imagine that Lois steals Peter's car. Because no one suspects Lois of this crime, she suffers no legal repercussions. As luck would have it, however, a corrupt police officer falsely accuses Lois of stealing a boat. Because this police officer is able to cleverly frame her, Lois is quickly convicted and then sentenced to six months in prison. After Lois is released, the authorities figure out both that she was wrongly convicted of stealing a boat and that she stole Peter's car. If the authorities now want to imprison Lois for the car theft, does she have a right against this punishment on the grounds that she has already been wrongly punished for stealing the boat and thus any additional punishment would constitute impermissible overpunishment? I think so.[17]

Against this conclusion, one might insist that the punishments for these two thefts are distinct and must be kept separate. If Lois was framed for stealing the boat by an agent of the state, then presumably Lois has a moral claim against that agent (and perhaps the state as a whole) to compensation for the unjustly imposed hard treatment, but that does not mean that Lois has a right against being punished for other wrongs she may have committed. In other words, Lois may have a right to a substantial financial settlement, but she does not have a "punishment credit" that she can apply against other wrongdoing.

To see why I resist this response, notice that financial settlements are typically (relatively poor) substitutes for which we settle when the item wrongly taken cannot be returned or replaced. If Lois chops off Peter's arm, for instance, we might require Lois to financially compensate Peter for his loss because this is the best we can do, given that Lois is unable to reattach Peter's arm. Similarly, we sometimes financially compensate people who have been wrongly incarcerated because there is no way that we can literally give them back the time that they spent behind bars. In this case, however, the authorities *are* able to give time back, since the state can give Lois the six months of freedom she is owed from her wrongful imprisonment for stealing a boat by not incarcerating her for stealing Russ's car. In short, once one appreciates that Lois's claim to money is merely a second-best solution to which states resort in virtue of their inability to repay in kind victims of wrongful incarceration, there appears no reason to deny that Lois could have a claim against the state that she not be imprisoned.

Second, imagine that Lois steals Peter's car. Peter suspects that Lois is the thief and thus reports her to the authorities. Lois is able to convince the police that she is innocent, and so they elect not to prosecute her. Peter is not content to let Lois go unpunished, however, so he builds a private prison in his basement and incarcerates Lois for six months. After he releases Lois, she goes to the police and accuses Peter of kidnapping her. During their investigation into the matter, the police become convinced that Peter is correct: Lois did steal his car. The authorities then prosecute, convict, and sentence Lois to six months imprisonment for stealing Peter's car. Does Lois have a right against this punishment on the grounds that she has already been privately punished for stealing the car and thus any additional punishment would constitute impermissible overpunishment? I think so.

One might contest my judgment on various grounds. For instance, one might insist that only a state can punish.[18] This strikes me as patently false, though. After all, surely no one would deny that Peter is capable of punishing his children. A more sophisticated objection would be to insist that legitimate states enjoy a monopoly on justified criminal punishment, and thus (although Peter is *able* to punish Lois) he is not morally permitted to do so. This may be right. But even if the state has a right that ordinary citizens refrain from vigilante justice, this might entail only that Peter has violated his duty to the state (or his compatriots), not that Lois cannot claim that she has already been punished. Thus, while some would insist that Lois may now be entitled to sue Peter but has no claim against being punished by the state, I am more inclined to say that Lois has a right against any additional punishment for stealing Peter's car and the state has at most a claim against Peter for violating his duty to refrain from exercising vigilante justice.

Third, imagine that Lois steals Peter's car. Lois later feels guilty about her conduct and confesses her crime to the authorities. Because the police do not believe Lois, however, they decline to pursue the case against her. This only strengthens Lois's feelings of guilt, and so she decides to punish herself. Toward that end, she takes out an advertisement in the local paper condemning herself for stealing Peter's car and explaining that she is resigning from her job and confining herself to a homemade prison for six months. Unsurprisingly, this advertisement receives a fair amount of media attention, which in turn leads the authorities to take a second look at the case. Eventually, shortly after her self-imposed six-month sentence has been completed, the authorities prosecute, convict, and sentence Lois to six months imprisonment for stealing Peter's car. Does Lois have a right against this imprisonment on the grounds that she has already punished herself for stealing the car and thus any additional punishment would constitute impermissible overpunishment? I think so.

It is often regarded as axiomatic that one cannot punish oneself (or at least that putative self-punishment does not fully "count" as punishment). However, I am not sure that this is correct. And in this case, I am inclined to think that Lois may have a right against the state imposing a second, further punishment in response to her stealing Peter's car.

Fourth, imagine that Lois steals Peter's car, but no one ever suspects her of doing so. Shortly after she steals Peter's car, however, Glenn professes his love for Lois and asks her to marry him. When Lois politely declines, Glenn decides that "if he cannot have her, then neither will anyone else," and so he imprisons Lois in his basement. After six months, Lois is able to escape and proceeds directly to the authorities to report this crime against her. During the course of their investigation, the authorities discover that Lois stole Peter's car. Thus, in addition to prosecuting Glenn for kidnapping Lois, they prosecute, convict, and sentence Lois to six months in prison for stealing Peter's car. Does Lois have a right against this imprisonment on the grounds that she has already been punished by Glenn, and thus any additional punishment would constitute impermissible overpunishment? I do not think so.

Here, for the first time, I think that Glenn's kidnapping and Lois's crime are distinct and must be kept separate. I appreciate that Lois's six-month ordeal with Glenn would likely be far more traumatic than a comparable prison sentence (at least in any humanely run prison), but there is more to punishment than hard treatment. In particular, it strikes me as clearly inappropriate to regard Lois's imprisonment by Glenn as punitive, because he had no knowledge of (and did not regard his actions as a response to) Lois's perceived wrongdoing. Thus, while Lois was undeniably treated horrifically by Glenn, she was not punished. Given this, Lois is in no position to conceive of the state's punishment as *additional* punishment, and thus cannot reasonably claim that the state's punishment constitutes *over*punishment.

Finally, imagine that Lois steals Peter's car. No one even suspects her of this crime. Shortly after Lois steals the car, though, her fancy high-tech house goes berserk when her smartphone (which controls every feature of her home) is struck by lightning. As a consequence, Lois is trapped in her kitchen. After six months, people in town start to notice that no one has seen Lois for quite some time, so they report her absence to the authorities. When the police come to Lois's house to investigate, they are able to liberate her. While there, however, they discover Peter's stolen car. The police thus prosecute, convict, and sentence Lois to six months in prison for stealing Peter's car. Does Lois have a right against this imprisonment on the grounds that she has already been punished by being trapped in her kitchen, and thus any additional punishment would constitute impermissible overpunishment? Again, I do not think so.

I recognize that Lois's ordeal was likely to have been traumatic, but unless we (implausibly) conceive of the lightning as sent by some divine being in response to Lois's crime, her confinement is clearly not punishment. Nature can make our lives more difficult, but it cannot punish us. As a consequence, Lois is in no position to complain that the state's punishment is either additional punishment or overpunishment.

One can of course contest my judgments about these five cases. For now, though, let us suppose that they are correct. What are we to make of this? It is noteworthy that the key difference between the first three cases and the last two is that, while Lois suffers hardship in all five, the hardship is deliberately imposed as a response to wrongdoing only in the first three. (Even in the case where Lois is framed, for instance, the hard treatment is meted out in response to *alleged* wrongdoing.) Thus, while Lois endures hardship in all five cases, she is *punished* in only the first three. This suggests the possibility that a wrongdoer does not forfeit her right against hard treatment; more specifically, she forfeits her right against *being punished*, where punishment is inherently responsive to wrongdoing.[19] If so, then the forfeiture is limited to certain, related reasons. Or more accurately, while those morally responsible for unjust threats may forfeit their rights against force for unlimited reasons, wrongdoers forfeit their rights only against hard treatment imposed for reasons related to the wrongdoing. In short, criminals forfeit their rights against only punishment, not hard treatment more broadly.

Before exploring this idea further, let me emphasize how it enables me to counter the objection that I am merely making an ad hoc move in order to save the forfeiture theory of punishment from some apparently counterintuitive implications. In particular, I have not merely *stipulated* that, while we should adopt an unlimited-reasons approach to overridden rights, waived rights, and rights forfeited by those responsible for unjust threats, we should endorse a limited-reasons account of the rights wrongdoers forfeit. Rather, I noted my independent conviction that a wrongdoer has a valid claim against overpunishment only if the hard treatment she endured was imposed for the right type of reasons. More specifically, a wrongdoer can plausibly allege that she has already been punished only if she has been subjected to hard treatment in response to (at least alleged) wrongdoing. If this is correct, we should conclude that there is a special connection between punishment and the types of reasons invoked by the agent who metes out the hard treatment, and this observation in turn provides at least some credence for the conclusion that wrongdoers do not forfeit their rights to be subjected to hard treatment for unlimited reasons.

Let us now explore the implications this analysis has for Simmons's Butch, Nozick's sadist, and a hybrid between the two. Recall that Butch roams the state of nature, looking for random victims to maim. He kills one person who, unbeknownst to Butch, has committed such a horrific wrong that she is morally liable to being painfully capitally punished. My new view is that Butch is not only deplorably vicious, he acts impermissibly. As I suggested all along, Butch's character is revealed to be horribly flawed by his willingness to painfully kill people who (for all he knows) are perfectly innocent. To this character assessment I can now add that Butch acts impermissibly, even though his victim has forfeited her right against being capitally punished, because Butch executes his victim for reasons that are entirely unrelated to her wrongdoing.

Nozick's sadist—call her Sadie—is someone who roams the state of nature on the lookout for unpunished wrongdoers.[20] While others spend their free time reading, hanging out in cafes, or surfing the web, Sadie enjoys nothing more than doling out punishments to those who have forfeited their rights against hard treatment. She is not necessarily proud of her appetite for inflicting pain, but she regards herself as resolutely committed to justice, and she (correctly) boasts that she has never punished an innocent person or overpunished a wrongdoer. Sadie strikes me as morally akin to the members of Kamm's Baby Killer Nation, and I would say that, while Sadie's character seems mixed (her sadism is deplorable while her commitment to justice is admirable), she does not act impermissibly.

Things become more difficult, though, if we imagine a cross between Butch and Sadie, whom I will call Speculative Sadist. Like Butch and Sadie, Speculative Sadist derives great joy from hurting others. Like Sadie, Speculative Sadist respects the demands of justice and thus does not want to mete out hard treatment on anyone unless she is an unpunished (or at least underpunished) wrongdoer. And like Butch, Speculative Sadist wants to roam the state of nature and inflict pain on random unsuspecting victims. Speculative Sadist designs a strategy to satisfy her sadistic appetite without acting unjustly; she decides to prey upon only adults who are at least thirty years old. Speculative Sadist restricts herself in this way because she reasons that, while the average child may not have committed too many substantial sins, virtually all adults have surely committed many wrongs that have gone either un- or underpunished. Thus, Speculative Sadist says something like the following before she harms each of her victims: "I confess that I have no idea what in particular you have done wrong, but I am extremely confident that over the course of your life you have culpably violated many rights without being appropriately punished, and so I hereby permissibly harm you for that reason."[21] Finally, let us suppose that, while Speculative Sadist has no way of knowing this herself, every one of the many people she has ever attacked had in fact forfeited her rights against at least the punishment inflicted by the Speculative Sadist. How should we morally evaluate Speculative Sadist? What should we say about her character, and has she acted impermissibly?

Speculative Sadist's character is a mixed bag. She deserves credit for the extent to which she is concerned about violating the rights of others, but her desire to harm others is clearly a vice, and (even if she is lucky enough to harm no one who has not gone un- or underpunished) it is deplorable that she is willing to *risk* wronging others in such a speculative fashion. The really interesting question, though, is whether the Speculative Sadist has acted impermissibly. Unlimited-reasons forfeiture theorists will obviously say no, but there is room for intramural debate among limited-reasons theorists. What we might call "*broadly* limited-reasons" theorists will say that Speculative Sadist has acted permissibly. On their view, as long as (1) the person punished has forfeited her rights, (2) she is not subjected to disproportionately hard treatment, and (3) the punisher believes that the person punished has forfeited her right against this hard treatment, then it is an act of permissible punishment. "Narrowly limited-reasons" theorists will see things differently. On this alternate view, it is not enough that the punisher has a general belief that the person punished has forfeited her right against being punished; the punisher must know the particular wrong committed by the person she punishes.

There are three questions we should ask in evaluating the broadly and narrowly limited-reasons approaches. First, bearing in mind the distinction between impermissible and suberogatory acts, do we think that Speculative Sadist violated moral duties when she imposed hard treatments upon random adults in the state of nature, or is it truer to our moral phenomenology to say that, although this behavior turned out to be permissible (because all of her victims had in fact forfeited the requisite rights), it merely reflected badly on her character? Second, if a third party was present when Speculative Sadist was inflicting this pain, and if she knew that this particular victim had in fact forfeited his rights against being punished, would it be permissible for this third party to coercively defend this person being punished against Speculative Sadist's attack? Third and finally, would those who were subjected to Speculative Sadist's hard treatment have a right against subsequent punishment for their wrongdoing on the grounds that this additional punishment would constitute overpunishment, given that they had already been punished by Speculative Sadist? Those who are confident that (1) Speculative Sadist acts permissibly, (2) third parties may not permissibly interfere with Speculative Sadist's imposition of hard treatment, and (3) those subjected to Speculative Sadist's hard treatment have acquired a right against additional punishment endorse the *broadly* limited-reasons approach, whereas those who are convinced that (1) Speculative Sadist not only has a bad character but acts impermissibly, (2) third parties may permissibly interfere with Speculative Sadist's attacks, and (3) those who have endured Speculative Sadist's hard treatment have not acquired any new rights against future punishments favor the *narrowly* limited-reasons approach.

I must confess that I am more confident that these are the questions we should be asking than about particular answers to them. I am inclined to say that Speculative Sadist acts permissibly, third parties may not permissibly interfere with her, and those who are harmed by her are entitled to claim that they have already been punished for their wrongdoing, but I know of no arguments against someone who answers all three of these questions differently, and so I must conclude that the choice between broadly and narrowly limited-reasons accounts is a matter about which reasonable people can disagree.

CONCLUSION

My conclusions in this chapter are by far the most tentative of the book, but I am relatively confident in the following three conclusions. First, given the plausibility of an objectivist account of obligation, and given that an agent's reasons for acting do not determine the deontic status of her act when rights are overridden, waived, or forfeited in other contexts, we cannot summarily rule out the plausibility of the unlimited-reasons version of the rights forfeiture theory of punishment. In other words, what critics have labeled the "problem" of relatedness is better thought of as the "question" of relatedness. Second, our convictions about when a recipient of hard treatment can claim a right against additional punishment helps to clarify the nature of punishment, which in turn enables us to counter the charge that our move to a limited-reasons account is merely an ad hoc stipulation. Third and finally, as the case of Speculative Sadist illustrates, even those who endorse the limited-reasons approach might disagree about how broadly or narrowly the agent's reasons must be limited.

Chapter 7

Mala Prohibita

Rights forfeiture theory appears particularly well suited to explain the permissibility of punishing those who commit *mala in se* crimes.[1] It is much less clear, however, whether this account leaves sufficient normative space for *mala prohibita* crimes. In particular, assuming that one does not forfeit any rights unless one violates someone else's right, forfeiture theorists who want to defend a state's right to punish those who commit *mala prohibita* crimes must explain whose rights are violated by the commission of these crimes. I attempt to provide such an explanation here.

This chapter is divided into four sections. First I briefly explain why the category of *mala prohibita* presents a problem for rights forfeiture theorists.[2] Next I suggest how a forfeiture theorist might attempt to solve this problem. In the third section, I grapple with difficult questions about how severely one may be punished for committing a *mala prohibitum* act. And finally, I comment briefly on what rights and duties stem from unjust *mala prohibita* laws.

THE PROBLEM OF *MALA PROHIBITA*

Mala prohibita crimes raise difficult questions for forfeiture theorists who believe that one does not forfeit any rights unless one violates (or at least attempts to violate) a right because, unlike in the case of *mala in se* crimes, it is not obvious whose right the criminal violates. Compare, for instance, the *mala in se* crime of driving recklessly to the *mala prohibita* crime of driving on a public road without a valid vehicle registration sticker displayed in the legally required spot on one's front windshield.[3] It seems clear that reckless drivers violate the rights of others by exposing them to unacceptable risks, but whose right is violated by one's failure to display a vehicle registration sticker on one's car? In the same vein, compare the more complicated cases of Rape and Statutory Rape. In rape, a thirty-year-old man forces at gunpoint a thirty-year-old woman to have sex. In Statutory Rape, a thirty-year-old man has "consensual" sex with a seventeen-year-old girl in a jurisdiction that criminally prohibits men older than twenty from having sex with girls under the age of eighteen.[4] The case of Rape poses no special problems for the rights forfeiture account; given that Rapist clearly violated the rights of his victim, it follows straightforwardly that he has forfeited his right not to be punished. But the case of Statutory Rapist is more difficult. To see why, it is helpful to step back and consider the rationale behind statutory rape laws.

I presume that statutory rape legislation is typically motivated by the recognition that one's consent is morally valid only if one is sufficiently mature. If one is not mature enough to intellectually understand and/or emotionally appreciate all of the stakes involved in a given situation, then we do not think that one's consent is morally valid in this arena. If a five-year-old girl agrees to have sexual intercourse with me if I buy her some candy, for instance, the fact that she appears to "consent" to the sex is of no moral consequence whatsoever.[5] Although we may have to provide a slightly different explanation of why it is wrong for me to have sex with this young girl, it clearly seems just as wrong as the rapist who forces himself on his victim at gunpoint. In light of this, it is altogether understandable that states would criminally prohibit even what might appear to be consensual sex with those who are not mature enough for their "consent" to be morally valid. Given how difficult it would be to conclusively determine whether any specific person is (or was) in fact sufficiently mature, states understandably seek to avoid these foreseeable administrative difficulties by using age as a proxy for maturity. Thus, a statute prohibiting sex with someone under a certain age is typically utilized as a workable solution to the problem in question. When a jurisdiction insists that a man over the age of twenty may not have sex with a girl under the age of eighteen, for instance, it is thought that this formulation will enable the law to come acceptably close to ensuring that no girls who are insufficiently mature will have their rights violated by what might appear to be consensual sex. In addition, setting a clear age limit enables us to avoid worries about punishing people for violating excessively vague laws, the boundaries of which are difficult for even a conscientious citizen to discern. If the law clearly states that statutory rape involves a man over twenty having sex with a girl under the age of eighteen, for instance, then men can ensure that they will not be liable to punishment merely by refraining from having sex with anyone under the age of eighteen.[6]

In any event, the crucial point is that the age components of statutory rape laws are administrative tools designed to *approximate* rather than *perfectly track* maturity levels. Thus, when legislators pass a law prohibiting sex with girls under the age of eighteen, everyone recognizes that there is no magical psychological transformation that occurs on one's eighteenth birthday; many girls will be sufficiently mature well before that date, and some remain insufficiently mature long after they turn eighteen. Interesting questions can be raised about both of these types of case, but for my purposes here, problems emerge for those girls who are sufficiently mature before they turn eighteen. In particular, notice that Statutory Rapist may have consensual sex with a seventeen-year-old girl who is in fact sufficiently mature to give her morally valid consent to this sexual intercourse.

But if so, it seems as though Statutory Rapist did not violate any of his sexual partner's rights. And if we do not forfeit any rights without violating someone else's rights, Statutory Rapist does not appear to have forfeited any of his rights. The forfeiture theorist thus appears unable to explain why the Statutory Rapist may permissibly be punished.

There seem to be three salient options here: one could (1) deny that states may permissibly punish *mala prohibita* criminals, (2) deny that one forfeits rights only when one violates a right, or (3) provide an explanation as to why one violates rights when one breaks *mala prohibita* laws. I regard (3) as the most promising alternative, and I shall pursue this option at length below. Still, it is worth briefly surveying the first two options, because, while I suspect that most would be considerably more receptive to the second option, I actually think (1) is more defensible than (2).

To appreciate why one may plausibly deny that the state may permissibly punish *mala prohibita* criminals, notice that not all rights forfeiture theorists are statists. Most take it for granted that the state is the party who will be doling out punishment, but not all forfeiture theorists presume that this must be so. Recall the positions of John Locke and John Simmons, for instance. Locke is a rights forfeiture theorist who believes that everyone in the state of nature has a competitive right to punish and the state acquires its exclusive executive right only when each of us voluntarily agrees for the state to have sole authority over this domain. Simmons agrees entirely with this normative picture, but, unlike Locke, he denies that existing states have in fact garnered the requisite consent from all of their constituents. Thus, without abandoning his rights forfeiture theory of punishment, Simmons denies that any existing state has an exclusive right to preside over the criminal legal system. In other words, Simmons believes that when it comes to punishing wrongdoers, existing states have merely the same competitive right as the rest of us.

Against this backdrop, consider the theorist who denies that states may permissibly punish *mala prohibita* criminals. In particular, notice that, while this position leaves considerably less room for state discretion over the criminal law than many presume is warranted, it does not amount to anarchism. A critic of *mala prohibita* crimes might well believe that existing states enjoy exclusive moral dominion over the punitive process; she will merely insist that criminal law must contain itself to *mala in se* crimes. Put in terms of my earlier example, for instance, this theorist does not object to the state's having exclusive authority to punish those men who have sex with insufficiently mature girls; she alleges only that the state may not punish all men who have sex with girls under a certain age *specified by the state*. A theorist of this stripe can therefore remain a statist because she need not object to the state's claiming a monopoly on punishment; she questions only the permissibility of a state's enacting laws with age limits that can result in men who have not in fact had sex with an insufficiently mature girl being punished as if they had done so.

Let me stress that I am not suggesting that this position is correct. On the contrary, my own view is that this stance leaves too little room for a legitimate state's discretion over the criminal law. The two points I seek to emphasize here are merely that it is neither incoherent nor incompatible with statism to deny that states may permissibly punish *mala prohibita* criminals, and that, even if forfeiture theorists were forced to adopt this position, it would not necessarily show that rights forfeiture theory should be rejected. It may instead be that viewing this issue through the lens of forfeiture theory shines a light on why and in what ways *mala prohibita* legislation is objectionable.

Turning to (2), many theorists are likely to be attracted to the idea that one can forfeit a right without violating (or at least attempting to violate) the rights of another. After all, there is more to morality than rights and their corresponding duties, so it seems obvious that one can behave deplorably without violating anyone's rights. To return to an earlier example: If the person in line behind me at the market is purchasing only one item (medicine for the sick twin infants she is struggling to pacify, perhaps), this may not entitle her to move ahead of me, but it nonetheless seems plausible to say that I ought to offer to let her go first. In other words, while I may be well within my rights to insist upon my position in front of her, I would clearly be displaying a vice if I either failed to notice this struggling mother's plight or, even worse, recognized her situation but was unmoved by it.

I agree, but I still think that one retains one's right not to be punished unless one violates someone else's right. As I stressed in the introduction, I believe that one can behave deplorably without acting impermissibly. The best way to characterize the behavior of someone who insists upon her right to remain in front of the weary mother at the market is in terms of the suberogatory, a category of behavior that, though not forbidden by duty, nonetheless reflects badly on an agent. The important point for my purposes here, though, is that it seems natural to think that one is not morally liable to punishment unless one acts *impermissibly*; we may criticize but not punish those who act in a suberogatory fashion. I believe this stance is confirmed by reflecting on cases like my contemptible behavior at the market. That is, while I certainly believe that it is appropriate for others to deplore and even criticize my behavior, it seems wrong to say that anyone might permissibly punish me. And the best explanation for this judgment, I think, is that one remains morally immune to punishment as long as one acts permissibly, where the bounds of permissibility are set by the rights of others.

I would like to think that my discussion of sadism and gratuitous harming in chapter 2 has helped to motivate this position, but I must concede that I have no irrefutable argument against someone with opposing convictions. In other words, I have no way of conclusively rebutting someone who thinks that I may permissibly be punished for failing to let the weary mother go ahead of me even though she had no right to do so. Because my stance on this issue makes it more rather than less difficult for the forfeiture theorist to contend with *mala prohibita* laws, however, I am comfortable simply asserting without further argument that one forfeits one's right not to be punished only if one violates (or at least attempts to violate) a second party's rights. And given this assumption, a forfeiture theorist who seeks to defend *mala prohibita* crimes must explain how those who commit these crimes violate someone else's rights. In the next section, I shall explore the possibility that *mala prohibita* criminals violate the rights of their compatriots when they break a just law of a legitimate state.

WHY *MALA PROHIBITA* CRIMINALS VIOLATE RIGHTS

Framing the issue of a state's right to enact *mala prohibita* legislation in terms of the anarchism/statism debate as I did above is illustrative, because it suggests that the promise of explaining the permissibility of punishing *mala prohibita* criminals is connected to a citizen's obligation to obey the law. In particular, if one's compatriots have a right that one obey the law, then perhaps the best way for a forfeiture theorist to explain why a *mala prohibita* criminal may permissibly be punished is because, in disobeying the law, the criminal has violated the rights of her compatriots. With this in mind, let me quickly explain why there is a moral duty to obey the law.

The first question is, Why be a statist? After all, given that states coerce everyone within their territorial boundaries, we must begin with a strong presumption in favor of anarchism. As I outlined in chapter 3, I am a statist because I believe that states are permitted (indeed, obligated) to impose themselves upon their constituents because this imposition is necessary to provide crucial benefits that would be unavailable in their absence, and I believe that states can supply these benefits without imposing unreasonable costs upon their constituents. As political theorists have long emphasized, it would be virtually impossible to pursue rewarding projects and nurture meaningful relationships unless everyone within a territorial district adhered to a common, clearly promulgated, and impartially adjudicated set of rules. And since states seem necessary to secure an environment in which everyone can count on each other to defer to a common set of rules, states perform an incredibly important function that justifies their coercive presence.

Given that states perform their valuable functions by coordinating all of their constituents, it is tempting to conclude that each citizen has a duty to obey the law because her legal obedience is necessary for the production of the important benefits of political stability. But this inference is too quick. While it may be true that a state could not perform its justifying political functions unless *a sufficient number* of its constituents complied with this state's legal commands, a typical individual's legal obedience is clearly not essential to the state's capacity to secure the goods of political stability. My country's capacity to perform its vital functions will not be discernibly affected by whether or not I pay my taxes this year, for example. And if it is descriptively inaccurate to say that my legal obedience is necessary for the provision of the benefits of political stability, then we cannot explain an individual's duty to obey the law with the same straightforward consequential line that justifies the state as a whole. This does not mean that citizens have no duty to obey the law, of course, but it does highlight the need to invoke an additional, extraconsequential consideration. I believe this supplemental element is fairness. In my view, each citizen has a duty to obey the law as her fair share of the collective political task. Thus, if states are justified because they perform the incredibly important task of rescuing all of us from the perils of the state of nature, then each of us has a duty to obey the law as her fair share of this larger communal project. And most important for my purposes here, someone who wrongly disobeyed the law would be treating her compatriots unfairly. Even if there were no discreet harms that followed from her legal disobedience, she would be taking unfair advantage of her fellow citizens.

I have developed and defended this account of political obligation at some length elsewhere, but I shall not say any more about the details of this approach here, so that I can return to the question of whether this account of the duty to obey the law can help illuminate why *mala prohibita* criminals necessarily violate rights.[7] I shall return to the example of statutory rape laws below, but let me start with a couple of easier cases: the requirements that drivers neither (1) exceed the posted speed limit nor (2) drive a vehicle without a valid vehicle registration sticker on its front windshield.

Before analyzing the requirement that I not drive faster than sixty-five miles per hour on a given stretch of highway, it is important to highlight that one can violate another person's rights without actually injuring her. If my reckless driving causes me to run into another person, then obviously I have violated this person's rights. But I can also violate another's rights without actually colliding into anyone else, because others have a right against being exposed to unreasonable risk of harm. And because the risk one poses to others is a function of the speed at which one drives, there is nothing terribly problematic about saying that one can violate the rights of others by driving too fast. Even if I am lucky enough to hit no one as I speed through a crowded intersection at one hundred miles per hour, for instance, I have still violated the rights of those people in the vicinity. But while this reasoning might seem to justify the state's enforcing designated speed limits, this inference does not automatically follow. In particular, note that there is a huge difference between a state's criminally prohibiting reckless driving in general and its criminally prohibiting driving over the speed of sixty-five miles an hour on a given stretch of road. The problem, of course, is that there will presumably be many cases in which one can safely exceed this speed limit (perhaps by a considerable margin) without exposing others to unreasonable risks. And if the state punished a professional race car driver like Danica Patrick for driving ten miles over the posted speed limit when (given the quality of her car and her extraordinary driving skills) she could in fact have driven considerably faster without posing unacceptable risks on others, it appears as though the state is punishing her when she has not violated the rights of others. And since we are assuming both that (1) one cannot forfeit one's rights without violating anyone else's rights, and (2) one may not permissibly be punished unless one has forfeited one's right against this hard treatment, this routine case of *mala prohibitum* punishment appears unjust.

But if the state has a right to impose the more specific legal requirement that no one exceed sixty-five miles per hour on this particular stretch of road, and all of the state's citizens owe it to each other to obey laws such as this, then perhaps the punishment would be justified after all because, by violating her compatriots' rights that she obey the law, Danica forfeited her right against being punished. With this in mind, the crucial question is why a state might permissibly require that no one drive faster than sixty-five miles per hour when, before this legal pronouncement, everyone had only the more general duty not to expose each other to excessive risks. And the answer here presumably features the great benefits that come with having a publicly known and uniformly enforced specification of what speed everyone must treat as excessively risky.

Among the basic ideas here is the well-known worry about the harms that would foreseeably ensue if each of us was left to interpret for herself what speed is required by the more general injunction against exposing others to unacceptable risks. Given the room for reasonable disagreement about the specifics here, our roads would be much less safe, there would be many more accidents, and the arguments over who was responsible for these accidents would be considerably more frequent and intractable. If this is right, it seems plausible to conclude not only that the state may permissibly impose speed limits but also that each citizen owes it to her compatriots to obey these limits. If a citizen exceeds the designated speed limit, then she is not doing her fair share to contribute to the benefits that these laws provide, and thus is violating the rights of her compatriots. In other words, each of us is morally prohibited from exposing others to unreasonable risks, but being part of a political community can also require one to refrain from relying solely on one's personal judgment as to which risks are in fact excessive. The duty not to expose others to unreasonable risks is owed to all other *humans*, and the duty to defer to the state's uniformly imposed assessment of which particular risks are unacceptable is owed to one's *compatriots*.[8]

The legal requirement that one not drive a vehicle without a registration sticker on its front windshield is in some ways distinct from speeding laws because, whereas the prohibition against exceeding sixty-five miles per hour corresponds to the general right others have not to be exposed to unreasonable risk, others would seem to have no rights to your affixing stickers anywhere. Nonetheless, I think a similar justification can be given. Notice, for instance, that the quality of one's car is among the factors that affect the level of risk one's driving poses to others. If the brakes on one's car did not work well, for example, then your driving at the legally posted speeds might well pose unreasonable risks to others. Given this, there seems nothing illegitimate about a state's prohibiting people from driving unsafe cars on public roads. And if the state is going to enforce this legal requirement, it does not seem objectionably demanding for it to require that drivers periodically confirm that their vehicles are in fact roadworthy. Finally, in order for the state to actually oversee this issue without prohibitive administrative costs, the state might require drivers to publicly display evidence that their cars have passed the requisite tests by placing a sticker in the designated spot on the car. Thus, while others initially have nothing like a right that one affix stickers on one's windshield, once a state requires that drivers demonstrate the safety of their vehicles in this fashion, it seems plausible that citizens acquire a duty to do so.

If the foregoing arguments are on target, then perhaps the fact that we have a duty to obey the law—a duty that is owed to our compatriots—enables a rights forfeiture theorist to explain why someone may permissibly be punished for driving faster than sixty-five miles per hour or in a car that does not have the requisite registration sticker affixed to its front windshield. One might worry, however, that this explanation proves too much. In particular, if someone may permissibly be punished merely for breaking the law, does this not give the government a blank check to punish any behavior whatsoever, as long as it criminally prohibits it first? This is an important objection. As much as we might hope to justify punishing *mala prohibita* crimes, it certainly does not seem permissible for a state to punish people for putative "crimes" such as failing to wear last week's dirty underwear on their heads, even if the state enacted clear prospective laws requiring everyone to do so. To avoid this criticism, we need some principled way of distinguishing those *mala prohibita* laws whose violators we can legitimately punish from those whose violators we cannot. The most natural place to draw this distinction, I would presume, is between just and unjust *mala prohibita* laws. And if this is right, we may permissibly punish someone for driving in excess of the posted speed limit while we may not punish those who fail to wear last week's dirty underwear on their heads because the former law is just while the latter is unjust.

Although this solution appears promising, critics may object that it saddles us with an unacceptable position regarding the duty to obey the law. In particular, if we suggest that one may permissibly be punished only for violating just *mala prohibita* laws, this must be because we have a moral duty to obey only just laws. But one's theory of political obligation cannot discriminate among laws according to whether or not they are just, because doing so is inconsistent with this duty being content-independent. Let me explain.

Not everyone believes that there is a duty to obey the law, but those who do typically distinguish between legitimate and illegitimate regimes and allege that we have duties to obey only the commands of the former. I agree that there is no general duty to obey the laws of an illegitimate state, but, as I have argued elsewhere, neither do we necessarily have an obligation to obey all of the commands of a legitimate state.[9] On my view, we have a general duty to obey only the just laws of a legitimate regime.

Now, some reject the conclusion that we have a duty to obey only the just laws of a legitimate regime, because they worry that it amounts to denying that we have content-independent reasons to obey the law. After all, critics opine, if the obligation to obey the law is to do any work, presumably it must be able to obligate us to do things we would not otherwise be morally required to do. But if we are obligated to obey only the just laws of a legitimate state, then it is the justice of the commands (rather than the fact that they are required by the state) that generates the duty. This objection misses the mark, however, because it presumes that all acts are either required by justice or prohibited by justice. This is a false dichotomy, though, because some acts are neither required nor prohibited; they are simply permissible acts that we are at liberty to do. Thus, those acts that are *required* by justice are a subset of just (i.e., permissible) acts. Given this, insisting that there is no obligation to obey an unjust law is perfectly compatible with there being content-independent reasons to obey the law. A traffic law requiring all drivers to drive on a particular side of the street, for instance, is but one example of a just law that might obligate citizens to do something that they would not otherwise be morally required to do.

This analysis is confirmed by our considered convictions regarding promising. Promising is typically regarded as a paradigmatic source of content-independent duties, since we routinely become obligated to do things that we would not otherwise be required to do (like meeting a friend for lunch) once we promise to do so. And notice: it is standardly supposed that promises to perform an injustice are null and void. That is, even if one promises to do X, one cannot have a duty to fulfill this promise if doing X is prohibited. But if our recognition that there is no duty to fulfill unjust promises is perfectly consistent with there being content-independent reasons to keep one's promises, why think that my contention that there is no obligation to obey unjust laws is incompatible with the existence of content-independent reasons to obey the just laws of a legitimate regime?

If this is right, then it would be permissible to punish *mala prohibita* criminals only if the particular laws they violated were just, and the reason that it seems perfectly reasonable to punish someone for driving faster than sixty-five miles per hour or for driving a car that has no registration sticker on its front windshield is that the state is justified in enacting each of these particular laws. With this in mind, let us return to the case of a statutory rape law that prohibits a man over the age of twenty from having sex with a girl under the age of eighteen. At first blush, the state's setting these age requirements looks no different from its setting speed limits: Just as the state sets a uniform speed of sixty-five miles per hour even though different drivers in various cars in distinct weather conditions can drive safely at dramatically different speeds, the state sets a uniform age of eighteen even though some girls will be sufficiently mature well before their eighteenth birthdays and others will not be mature enough until later. Despite these clear parallels, for three reasons we cannot infer the justice of a statutory rape law from the justice of a speeding limit. First of all, while safe driving conditions are adequately secured only if drivers are coordinated to drive at (roughly) the same speed, there is no comparable advantage to coordinating the age at which people have sex. Second, the punishment for statutory rape is typically dramatically more severe than the penalty for speeding, and so we should not be so quick to assume that we are not violating the rights of those punished for statutory rape. Third and less obviously, it may demand much more of a person to ask him to refrain from having sex with a given person than it does to ask him to avoid speeding. This claim may seem curious, but one must remember that not every man who wants to have sex with a girl under the age of eighteen is a despicable sexual predator. There is no reason that a man over the age of twenty cannot be deeply in love with a girl under the age of eighteen, and in these cases criminally prohibiting this couple from having sex is morally tantamount to prohibiting two gay men who love each other from having sexual relations.

Thus, even if a state violates no rights when it punishes all those who exceed a designated speed on any given stretch of road, it does not automatically follow that it similarly acts justly when it punishes all men over a given age who have sex with girls under a certain age. I will say more below about what I think a just statutory rape law would look like. For now, I will conclude more modestly by emphasizing only that the justifiability of any given *mala prohibita* law will depend upon a number of factors, including (1) the importance of the rights of the potential victims protected, (2) the severity of the punishment imposed, (3) the number and proportion of people punished who in fact committed no corresponding *mala in se* crime, and (4) the availability of alternative means of achieving the aims the particular law is designed to secure.

THE PROBLEM OF SENTENCING

If all of the foregoing arguments are sound, then a forfeiture theorist can explain why a legitimate state may permissibly punish someone guilty of committing a *mala prohibita* crime when the particular criminal statute is not unjust. Potential problems remain, however, because it is not clear that the forfeiture theorist can recommend appropriate sentences for all such crimes.

To see why the question of sentencing raises such difficult issues, let us return to the case of statutory rape. Because rape is such a horrific violation of the victim's rights, presumably it would be permissible to impose a correspondingly onerous punishment. But remember: In the cases of statutory rape, there is no guarantee that the presumptive victim's rights were in fact violated. If the legally underage girl was actually sufficiently mature, then her consent was morally valid, and the sex did not violate her rights. It does not follow that no one's rights were violated, however, since, as I argued above, the statutory rapist may have violated the rights of his compatriots by breaking a just law. And if the statutory rapist violated the rights of his compatriots, presumably he has forfeited his right not to be punished. But how much may he be punished?

As I acknowledged in chapter 2, I know of no algorithm that reliably generates specific answers to questions like this, but presumably one's compatriots' rights that one obey the law are not terribly weighty—certainly they are not as weighty as one's right not to be raped—and thus the statutory rapist may not permissibly be punished anywhere nearly as severely as the rapist. Because of this, justice apparently requires the state to punish a statutory rapist much less severely then it may punish a rapist. Putting this point in terms of admittedly arbitrary numbers that will be helpful simply for purposes of illustration, let us suppose that, while a rapist forfeits his right not be imprisoned for as many as ten years, a statutory rapist forfeits his right not to be imprisoned for no more than ten weeks. If so, it would be unjust for a state to punish statutory rapists for more than ten weeks.[10] This is problematic, however, because, while not all statutory rapists will have had sex with a girl who is insufficiently mature to have provided morally valid consent, many will have. And since these particular statutory rapists will have violated an extremely important right of those girls with whom they had sex, they will be woefully underpunished by any sentence that does not exceed ten weeks. Indeed, for those statutory rapists who had sex with an immature girl, an appropriate punishment would presumably be closer to ten years.

Thus, even if the arguments outlined in the previous section enable the rights forfeiture theorist to explain why *mala prohibita* criminals may be punished for committing crimes like statutory rape, they do not seem capable of providing acceptable answers to secondary questions that might be asked about sentencing. Interestingly, our analysis began with a worry about statutory rapists who had not violated the rights of their sexual partners being overpunished, but we now see that there is a more sophisticated worry about statutory rapists who have violated the rights of their sexual victims being underpunished. Combining these two observations, we can put the objection to forfeiture theory in the form of a dilemma: Statutory rapists might be sentenced to prison sentences of either ten weeks or ten years. If they are imprisoned for ten years, the state will be violating the rights of those statutory rapists whose sexual partners were mature enough to give their morally valid consent, but if they are imprisoned for only ten weeks, those statutory rapists whose victims were not old enough to give their morally valid consent will be dramatically underpunished.

Those familiar with the literature on the morality of punishment will likely notice that we have now stumbled onto a more localized version of an objection that is commonly invoked against what are often called "fairness" theories of punishment. Fairness theorists allege that punishment is justified because, by enjoying the benefits of everyone else's legal obedience and then breaking the laws themselves, criminals have taken advantage of the benefits of legal cooperation without contributing their fair share. This approach clearly has intuitive appeal, but most theorists reject it for two related reasons. First, in the case of many standard crimes, it offers a patently misguided account of the criminal's culpability. If Harry rapes Sally, for instance, Harry's moral liability to punishment presumably stems straightforwardly from his horrible mistreatment of Sally, rather than from some elaborate story about how Harry took unfair advantage of all of his compatriots who did their fare share by obeying the law against raping Sally. Put more succinctly, the punishment is warranted principally because Harry wronged Sally, not because he wronged his compatriots. And second, if a criminal's culpability is explained in terms of his taking unfair advantage of his compatriots, then we should punish Harry similarly regardless of whether he stole a pencil from Sally or raped her, because in both cases the wrong was the same: Harry took unfair advantage of his compatriots. But this seems crazy. Clearly Harry may permissibly be punished more for raping Sally than for stealing one of her pencils.

In general, forfeiture theory is strong where fairness theory is weak. Regarding *mala in se* crimes, the rights forfeiture account focuses on the victim's violated right, and, as a consequence, it supplies straightforward and compelling explanations as to why and how severely the criminal may be punished. The particular account of *mala prohibita* crimes I have developed in this chapter, however, is echoic of the fairness theory of punishment. It should therefore come as no surprise that I now face the same problem with sentencing of *mala prohibita* crimes that fairness theory faces more generally. Highlighting the ways in which my account of *mala prohibita* resembles the fairness theory of punishment also calls our attention to the prospect that the account defended here may sometimes misdiagnose why punishment is warranted. In particular, the punishable wrong committed by the statutory rapist who has sex with an insufficiently mature girl is presumably his violation of his victim's rights, not that he has somehow treated his compatriots unfairly. Thus, even if my account allows rights forfeiture theorists to explain why *mala prohibita* criminals may permissibly be punished, in some cases it offers a clearly misguided explanation that generates inappropriate recommendations for sentencing.

There may be no fully satisfactory solution to the dilemma of over- or underpunishing the distinct types of statutory rapists, but two salient options would be to (1) set the default punishment either at ten weeks and then allow the state to raise it as high as ten years in those cases where it can establish that the girl in question was in fact immature, or to (2) set the default punishment at ten years but provide an opportunity for the defendant to prove his innocence by establishing that the girl was mature enough to give her morally valid consent.[11] Neither option is ideal, but the second strikes me as more promising.

Setting the default punishment at the lower level of ten weeks and then evaluating the maturity of each girl in question has advantages (it would keep the burden of proof off of the defendant and help prevent overpunishment, for example), but it also seems problematic for several reasons.[12] First, the lesser sentence would not be much of a deterrent, and thus would not sufficiently protect prospective victims. Second, if the state determines that the apparent victim of a statutory rape was actually sufficiently mature, it is not clear that the statutory rapist should be punished at all. And third, states are motivated to utilize criminal legislation like statutory rape laws in order to avoid the administrative costs and complications of making these difficult psychological assessments in each and every case. Thus, requiring states to make these difficult judgments on the back end, after conviction but before sentencing, defeats at least one important purpose for which the laws were initially designed.

Given these problems, it might be better to set the default punishment at ten years and then build in institutional mechanisms that provide an opportunity for the defendant to prove his innocence if he can convince the court that the girl in question was sufficiently mature. Importantly, the statutory rapist should not be sentenced to the lesser charge of ten weeks if he can establish his innocence. Instead, I recommend that this mechanism should function similarly to self-defense. Just as a defendant who killed someone is not guilty and should not be sent to prison at all if she acted in self-defense, a man who had sex with a girl who was sufficiently mature to give her morally valid consent is not guilty and may not permissibly be sent to prison, even for ten weeks. One additional wrinkle that I would propose for statutory rape laws, though, would be that there should be some avenue available for girls to legally establish their maturity in advance of any potentially criminal action. I recognize that it may sound crazy to speak of girls under the designated age going to some state bureaucrat to apply for what essentially amount to licenses to have sex, but it seems to me that having this option would be an important improvement over the status quo. Imagine that a twenty-one-year-old Jack is in love with seventeen-year-old Jill in a jurisdiction that criminally prohibits men over the age of twenty from having sex with girls under the age of eighteen. If Jill and Jack want to have sex, and if Jill is in fact mature enough to give her morally valid consent, then one can imagine that they would be thrilled to have the opportunity to take the necessary steps to ensure that Jack would not be legally vulnerable to being imprisoned for ten years if they were discovered to have had sex. What is more, if a state provided such an opportunity, then it could without injustice set a weightier presumption that all girls under the age of eighteen are in fact insufficiently immature. In other words, if states provide ample opportunity for girls under the age of eighteen to antecedently establish their maturity, statutory rapist defendants have fewer grounds for complaint if they are subsequently saddled with a greater burden of proof to establish their innocence.

Finally, I recognize that requiring states to amend their laws in this fashion burdens them with additional costs, but it strikes me that these costs must be borne if states are to avoid egregious injustice. Having a criminal legal system in which killers can establish their innocence by demonstrating that they acted in self-defense also requires the legal system to be more costly and complicated, but no one doubts that these protections are required to ensure that innocent people are not wrongly punished. The only difference between our existing arrangements for self-defense and the amendments I am proposing for statutory rape laws, I would suggest, is that the issues surrounding *mala prohibita* legislation are less obvious than those attached to self-defense.

Of course, even if states sought to institute each of the changes I have recommended, such a system would inevitably make some mistakes, so we should expect that some men who had sex with insufficiently mature girls would wrongly escape punishment and others who had sex with girls who were mature enough would wrongly be sent to prison for ten years. But no legal system can be expected to work perfectly. The important point for my purposes here is that there appears to be no reason that a rights forfeiture theorist cannot plausibly defend *mala prohibita* criminal laws, even statutory rape legislation that attaches severe penalties to those duly convicted. As long as these laws provide adequate institutional mechanisms that enable those who have not in fact violated anyone's rights to establish their innocence, states are at liberty to construct their criminal laws with sharp, salient boundaries that admittedly only approximate actual guilt and innocence, even for crimes that carry substantial penalties.

THE INJUSTICE OF THE STATUS QUO

I have suggested that forfeiture theory is compatible with *mala prohibita* criminal laws, but I have also argued that justice requires that many existing *mala prohibita* laws be amended to provide greater assurances that innocent people are not wrongly punished. But the fact that my characterization of a just statutory rape law differs in important ways from many that are currently in existence raises additional questions. Specifically, given that I believe both that (1) one has a moral obligation to obey only the just laws of legitimate state, and that (2) many existing statutory rape laws are unjust, are those who are convicted under existing laws justly punished? And do they have a moral obligation to accept their punishment? My answer is: "It depends." More specifically, it depends upon whether the girl with whom the convicted criminal had sex was in fact insufficiently mature to give her morally valid consent. If the girl was not in fact mature enough, then the man did violate her rights, he forfeited his own right not to be punished, and there is no injustice in the state sending him to jail for an extended period. In this case, I believe that the injustice of statutory rape law is not germane, and the man may not forcibly resist his punishment. If the girl was sufficiently mature, however, then the man did not violate her rights, and he did not forfeit his right not to be punished. And because the statutory rape law does not provide the requisite mechanism for the defendant to establish his innocence, it is a seriously unjust law. And just as it would be wrong for a state to punish someone who killed in self-defense if this state gave defendants no opportunity to establish that they had acted in self-defense, it would be wrong for this state to punish a statutory rapist for anything like ten years. And finally, since there is no obligation to obey an unjust law, the statutory rapist whose sexual partner was in fact sufficiently mature has no moral obligation to accept his punishment.

CONCLUSION

Even those readers who disagree with nothing in this chapter might worry about the lengths to which I have had to go in order to show why forfeiture theory is compatible with punishing *mala prohibita* acts. Should the twin facts that I have had to work so hard and that *even then I have not been able to justify the status quo* lead us to be suspicious of rights forfeiture theory? I think not. Even though most who work on the morality of punishment take *mala prohibita* for granted and are anything but receptive to the rights forfeiture theory of punishment, I regard the difficulty we have had squaring this approach to punishment with existing *mala prohibita* laws as more of a reason to question the latter than the former. I say this for two reasons. First, with the possible exception of fairness theories of punishment (which famously have problems with *mala in se* crimes), I suspect that all but the crudest consequentialist approaches will have comparable difficulty with *mala prohibita*. In particular, any theory that includes deontological elements will insist that no one may permissibly be punished unless they do something wrong, and thus virtually all approaches will face similar difficulties capturing why those who commit *mala prohibita* crimes necessarily act wrongly. And second, if there are problems with the core arguments in this chapter, this spells trouble for my account of political obligation, not the rights forfeiture theory of punishment. As Daniel McDermott observes:

> Demonstrating that the state has the right to punish, and in particular that it has the right to punish acts that are *mala prohibita*, is the task of a theory of political obligation. It is only once the state occupies that position of special moral authority claimed by proponents of theories of political obligation that it even makes sense to discuss such acts as *wrongdoing*. Whereas the task of a justification of punishment is to explain why punishment is the just response to moral wrongdoing, the task of a theory of political obligation is to explain why acts that are *mala prohibita* are in fact instances of moral wrongdoing.[13]

Following McDermott, I suggest that, even if other authors could supply better accounts of political obligation than I have in this chapter, this gives us no reason to reject rights forfeiture theory. And if my arguments have been on target, the enduring lesson of this chapter is that even legitimate states do not enjoy as much political authority as they claim, and thus we should be suspicious of how freely and generously existing states help themselves to *mala prohibita* legislation.

Chapter 8

No One Defends the Status Quo

There is a healthy debate between abolitionists and retentionists. Abolitionists object that the deliberate hard treatment of punishment cannot be justified, while retentionists insist that there are circumstances in which punishment is morally permissible.[1] It is important to recognize, however, that, while the vast majority of those who work on punishment are retentionists, *no one* defends the status quo. Indeed, criminal legal systems in countries like the United States are considered by some to be so bad that the state's very legitimacy is called into question. The most obvious way to press this claim is in terms of the death penalty.[2] Many lament that the United States is the only "civilized" country that continues to engage in the "barbaric" practice of capital punishment. And given the existence of a human right to life, critics suggest that any state that resorts to capital punishment is obviously violating the human rights of its own constituents.

I am no cheerleader for the death penalty, but I have never been convinced by this line of critique. There is unquestionably a moral human right to life, but it is not clear why this right cannot be forfeited. I have no conclusive argument that the right to life *can* be forfeited, but it seems illegitimate to say that someone is necessarily unreasonable merely because she believes that a murderer, say, can forfeit her right to life. Against this, it is sometimes alleged that human rights cannot be lost. After all, no matter how horrifically one acts, one never ceases to be human. As James Nickel has observed, however, this argument cannot be sound, because it implausibly implies that all countries that incarcerate criminals are illegitimate.[3] This is because imprisoning someone who has done nothing wrong would also violate her human rights, so unless one can forfeit one's human right against being imprisoned, all existing countries would be illegitimate. It clearly seems more plausible to suppose that regimes that incarcerate wrongdoers remain legitimate because the incarcerated criminals have forfeited their human rights against imprisonment. But if one can lose one's human right against being imprisoned, why cannot one similarly forfeit one's right against being killed? Thus, even though I would not hesitate to abolish the death penalty if I had power to do so, I do not think capital punishment necessarily violates human rights, and so I do not worry that the United States is automatically illegitimate because it capitally punishes criminals.

As radical as it sounds, I think a more promising line of critique against the United States' legitimacy would be to allege that its criminal legal system as a whole constitutes a widespread and systematic human rights atrocity. In defense of this claim, I want to focus on the quantity, nature, and distribution of wrongful imprisonment perpetrated by the US government. More specifically, I will argue that the (1) overcriminalization, (2) overpunishment, (3) horrific prison conditions, and (4) background social and economic injustice in the United States combine to constitute a widespread and systematic human rights atrocity.

OVERCRIMINALIZATION

The biggest problem with criminal law in the United States is its overreach. Many branches of government are prone to mission creep, but we should be especially concerned when criminal legal institutions expand beyond their appropriate proportions, because the result is that people are wrongly punished. The theorist who has done the most to call attention to this phenomenon is Douglas Husak. Husak argues that our criminal law has expanded in a variety of regrettable ways, but the issue on which he has written most extensively is the criminalization of recreational drugs. As he writes: "In 2004, approximately 1,745,000 persons were arrested for drug offenses in the United States. About 82% of these were arrested for simple possession. Over 410,000 drug offenders are in jails and prisons across the country—about the same number as the entire prison population in 1980. Nearly one of every five prisoners in America is behind bars for a nonviolent drug offense. This figure has climbed dramatically. In 1986, about 18 of every 100,000 American citizens were imprisoned for a drug offense; that ratio had jumped to 63 a decade later."[4]

But why think that a state may not permissibly punish someone for, say, possession of cocaine? As long as the state clearly and prospectively prohibits its possession, on what grounds can someone rightfully object to being punished? Husak emphasizes that punishment is the worst thing that a state can do to one of its citizens and that each of us has a right not to be punished unless she deserves this hard treatment. More specifically, he argues that it is impermissible to punish someone unless she deserves it for wrongful conduct that nontrivially harms others. I am broadly sympathetic to this line of thinking, but I would express it in terms of rights forfeiture. Given my belief that you may permissibly be punished only if you forfeit your right against this hard treatment, and that (with the exception of criminal attempts) you forfeit this right only if you violate someone else's right, it is no surprise that I join Husak in strenuously objecting to the criminal prohibition of drugs. Imagine that I use cocaine recreationally, for instance. This habit may be neither laudable nor prudent, but, absent special circumstances (as when I promise my wife that I will not do drugs, for instance), it is hard to see how anyone else's rights could be violated by my free and informed drug use. Put bluntly, why is it anyone's business what I snort up my nose?

Here a defender of the current drug laws might respond that, even if there is nothing inherently objectionable about recreational drug use within the privacy of one's own home, the moral dynamics change when a legitimate state prohibits drugs. Because we owe it to our fellow citizens in a legitimate state to obey the law, others acquire a right that we refrain from using cocaine if the law prohibits its use. The core idea here is that a political state is able to perform its incredibly important functions of securing peace and protecting human rights only if we all respect its authority to unilaterally establish a clear and uniform set of rules. As a consequence, morality requires that we all obey the law as our fair share of the collective project of securing a just and peaceful society. Those who disobey the law thus wrong their compatriots by failing to do their fair share.

I like this account of the duty to obey the law, but as I outlined in my discussion of *mala prohibita,* I worry that this rendition exaggerates the moral authority of legitimate states. Because widespread vigilantism would invariably create a dangerous environment in which human rights are terribly insecure, I appreciate the desirability of states' having dominion over the criminal legal process. It thus strikes me as plausible that each of us has a moral duty to refrain from vigilantism, even when she is convinced that the state has failed to adequately punish those who have violated her rights. This line of thinking does not justify, however, the much more ambitious claim that a state may permissibly criminalize any conduct whatsoever. In other words, even if each of us has a moral duty to support the state's efforts to prosecute and punish rights violators, it does not follow that the state is morally entitled to punish those who do not violate anyone's rights, even if it publicly warns citizens of its plans to do so. A state presumably has no right to criminalize people for wearing blue shirts on Tuesdays, for instance, even if it announces in advance that wearing blue shirts on Tuesdays will become a punishable offense. The pivotal idea here is that, just because we want the state to have unrivalled control over the prosecution and punishment of all suspected rights violators, it does not follow that the state thereby acquires an unlimited right to punish people for whatever conduct it chooses. And because wearing blue shirts on Tuesdays does not violate anyone else's rights, it seems an obvious injustice to punish anyone for doing so. But why not say the same thing about drug use? Given that doing cocaine in the privacy of one's own home no more violates anyone's rights than wearing a blue shirt on a Tuesday, the state has no right to criminalize such recreational drug use.

One might worry that my comparison between wearing a blue shirt and doing cocaine is inapt. Whereas the widespread wearing of blue shirts will not affect others, many rural communities have been decimated by meth use, and urban communities have been ravaged by crack use. Given that governments are responsible for ensuring that communities do not deteriorate in these ways, there seems nothing inappropriate about a state criminalizing the possession and use of drugs that inexorably lead to such a sad state of affairs. In other words, when the stakes are as high as this for entire communities, governments appear to have a legitimate interest in prohibiting the harmful behavior. And if they have such an interest, it is terribly misleading to compare laws that prohibit drug use to those that criminalize wearing blue shirts on Tuesdays.

I do not want to appear cavalier about the problems facing those communities struggling with drug epidemics, but it strikes me as illegitimate to cite existing problems to justify the current expansion of criminal law, because it seems more plausible to suppose that the increased criminalization is itself an integral part of the problem. Think about the US experience with the prohibition of alcohol, for instance. Alcohol abuse is obviously a huge psychological and health issue for individuals, families, and larger communities. When the commercial production and sale of alcohol was prohibited, however, communities often became far worse off, because of all of the issues surrounding criminalization. Most notably, organized crime became much more lucrative and sophisticated (and legal institutions became correspondingly more corrupt) when it was against the law to produce and sell alcohol. Thus, even if alcohol consumption decreased during prohibition, many people continued to drink (and thus continued to cause problems for themselves, their families, and their communities), and communities had the additional problems associated with organized crime. What is more, many lives were avoidably blighted by lengthy prison sentences. In view of this, not even those keenly aware of the dangers of alcohol abuse now recommend that we return to prohibition.

The same dynamic clearly seems to have occurred with the so-called war on drugs. Rather than eliminate recreational drug use, the existing legal structure has spawned criminal enterprises that undermine the very communities governments seek to protect. Not only is there an enormous amount of violence surrounding the drug trade, customers are often provided with unsafe drugs and not infrequently have their lives marred by (unnecessary) prison sentences. If the state legalized and then taxed the production, sale, and consumption of recreational drugs, it would thereby (1) eliminate the need for criminal suppliers, (2) be able to ensure that the drugs being sold were safer for consumption, and (3) use the tax revenue to fund solutions to whatever social problems arose. The government would also save the enormous amount it is currently spending to police, prosecute, and imprison the vast number of criminals associated with the illicit drug trade. And if it redirected just a small fraction of these savings to programs like early education and preventive healthcare for at-risk children, it is hard to imagine how the communities that the drug laws are purportedly designed to protect would not be dramatically better off. And most important, the state would no longer be criminally punishing people who have done nothing to render themselves morally liable to such hard treatment.[5] If this assessment is correct, then one cannot plausibly allege that drug laws are nothing like legislation that makes it illegal to wear blue shirts on Tuesdays on the grounds that the former are necessary for the health of imperiled communities when these very laws are playing a key causal role in the destruction of the communities in question.

Before closing this section, let me recapitulate this argument in terms of the distinction between *mala in se* and *mala prohibita* crimes. Even if we begin by assuming that legitimate states have a moral claim to exclusive control over the prosecution and punishment of *mala in se* crimes (as I believe we should), it does not follow that these regimes have unlimited discretion regarding *mala prohibita* crimes. It is always possible that someone could supply a compelling argument for why some states enjoy this type of sweeping moral authority, but no one to my knowledge has done so yet. In the absence of a convincing argument for this more general conclusion, each law that criminalizes conduct that is not inherently rights-violating must be justified on a case-by-case basis. There may be good arguments for some of the criminal prohibitions that the United States has adopted, but it is hard to see how the current drug laws could be justified. And if so, a great deal of what the United States currently prohibits may simply be unjustifiable mission creep. It follows that vast numbers of those presently detained in US prisons have done nothing to forfeit their rights against punishment and thus are having their human rights violated by a state merely because it has the power (but no moral right) to do so.

OVERPUNISHMENT

For the sake of argument, let us suppose that there is no problem with overcriminalization and that every inmate in US prisons has in fact violated someone else's rights. Even so, we should be concerned about overpunishment, because wrongdoers do not forfeit all of their rights; more minimally, they forfeit only their rights against a *proportionate* punishment.

To motivate this point about proportionality, imagine that I am trying to steal your umbrella. Given that it is your umbrella, you are well within your rights to forcibly resist my attempt to steal it. Presumably you would be permitted to shove or punch me, for instance, if this was necessary to prevent me from taking it. Suppose, however, that I am bigger and stronger than you, and that the only way you can effectively stop me from stealing your umbrella would be to shoot me. Would it be permissible for you to do so? What if you warned me first?

Even if you solemnly threatened to shoot me if I tried to steal your umbrella, it would be wrong for you to do so. The best way to capture this wrongness is in terms of proportionality: Shooting me to retain your umbrella is an objectionably disproportionate response because (even though the umbrella is indisputably yours) an umbrella is not valuable enough to justify such a great harm to me. In other words, while my attempt to steal your umbrella has left me morally liable to *proportionate* defensive force (and thus you would not violate my rights if you shoved or punched me), I am not liable to *all* possible defensive measures (and thus you would violate my rights if you shot me).

Proportionality constrains the permissibility of punishment in an analogous fashion. Imagine, for instance, that I successfully stole your umbrella. Because I have culpably violated your rights, I have thereby forfeited my rights against punishment. Would it be permissible to shoot me as punishment? Presumably not. Even if my wrongdoing has rendered me morally vulnerable to punishment, I am not liable to any punishment whatsoever. Put in terms of rights, shooting me as punishment for stealing your umbrella would violate my rights, because, while I have forfeited my rights against a proportionate punishment, I retain my right against being overpunished. And because shooting me is obviously a disproportionate response to my stealing an umbrella, a state that punished umbrella thieves by shooting them would violate these criminals' rights even if they announced this punishment in advance and made sure to shoot only those who had in fact stolen umbrellas.

In my view, those who are overpunished have their rights violated in the same way and for the same reasons as the innocent who are wrongly punished. If a criminal has forfeited her right against a one-year incarceration but is imprisoned for two years, for instance, then the second year in prison would be an impermissible overpunishment. As a psychological matter, we may typically be less moved by a guilty person's overpunishment than by an innocent person's wrongful punishment, but this unjustified second year of incarceration for the guilty person is just as objectionable as a one-year prison sentence for an innocent person.[6]

I presume that none of this is terribly controversial. Establishing that the United States routinely overpunishes criminals remains difficult, however, because—even if everyone acknowledges that criminals should not be disproportionately punished—there is plenty of room for reasonable disagreement about proportionality. Virtually everyone would concede that umbrella thieves should not be shot, for instance, but it is much less clear precisely when a prison sentence becomes disproportionately long. And what if I stole a whole truckload of umbrellas? Or what if this is the third time I have been caught stealing an umbrella?

One way to generate relatively precise answers to these questions is to appeal to the principle of *lex talionis,* the idea of an eye for an eye, a tooth for a tooth, and a life for a life. The rights forfeiture analog of this retributive principle specifies that a criminal forfeits the very same right she violates. Although this formula has the obvious virtue of simplicity, I fear that it is too simple. Among other things, it wrongly focuses exclusively on consequences. To see how and why this is so, notice that no one should be punished in the absence of both *actus reus* (a bad act) and *mens rea* (a guilty mind). If I poke your eye out when I sneeze, for instance, I should not be punished because I did not have the requisite culpability. It also seems clear that the severity of punishment should track both the badness of the act and the quality of the mental state. If Caroline *negligently* pokes an eye out, Jennifer *recklessly* pokes an eye out, and Kelly *maliciously* pokes an eye out, for example, then presumably Kelly is morally liable to a more severe punishment than Jennifer, who in turn may be punished more than Caroline. According to *lex talionis*, however, all three deserve the same punishment: having one of their own eyes poked out.

If we eschew the principle of *lex talionis* for the more general (and vague) stance that criminals forfeit their rights against a proportionate punishment, it becomes more difficult to specify precisely which convicts have been overpunished. Indeed, because the United States incarcerates rather than shoots people for stealing, and because there is room for reasonable people to disagree about which prison sentences "fit" which crimes, it is difficult for me to conclusively show that the United States overpunishes wrongdoers. It is not difficult, however, to point to features of the US political environment that support the conclusion that our current political climate is disposed to generate these objectionable results.

A popular explanation for the recent tendency to legislatively mandate excessive prison sentences is that they are being promoted by the so-called prison-industrial complex, those parties (such as towns where prisons are built and companies that build prisons and sell prison supplies) who profit from a growing prison population. The basic idea is that these various actors have united to successfully lobby on behalf of prison sentences that are considerably longer than one would ever recommend as proportionate.

I do not want to completely discount this theory, but I wonder if two other factors are not more influential. (After all, money can equally be made by those who would build and staff schools, and yet we hear very little about an "education-industrial complex.") First, it strikes me that the current media environment compels politicians to demonstrate that they are tougher on crime than their competitors. Both the local stations (whose newscasts should be entitled "Local weather, sports, and scary criminals") and the cable news outlets (who face constant pressure to fill their twenty-four-hour schedule with gripping content) have a financial interest in inspiring fear of crime. As a consequence, whenever a sensational crime is reported by the media, politicians rush to introduce new legislation that mandates increasingly draconian minimum prison sentences from which judges are not permitted to deviate. Second, there has been a recent proliferation of criminal charges that can be "stacked" against a defendant for committing what (used to be) a single crime. Politicians are motivated to create new crimes (like money laundering, which criminalizes the banal act of depositing money in the bank) in order to empower law enforcement authorities who have a difficult time convicting criminals. (After all, the most important members of organized criminal rings are seldom on the streets doing the dirty work.) Plus, when the charges against any given defendant are multiplied, this gives prosecuting attorneys additional leverage with which to negotiate plea deals that enable them to avoid both the expense of going to trial and the risks associated with trying to secure a conviction.

Given that those running for public office stand no chance of being (re)elected if their opponents can portray them as "soft on crime," and given the understandable urge of those in office to empower our legal authorities with the tools (they claim) they need to fight crime, the temptation to create many of these new laws is neither mysterious nor necessarily malicious. But the cumulative effect of all of this legislation is the proliferation of new crimes and a collection of sentencing guidelines that no one would recognize as remotely proportionate. And this result is not the least bit surprising, because these laws are almost never conceived with an eye to ensuring that no one is overpunished.

HORRIFIC PRISON CONDITIONS

It is commonly lamented how psychologically destructive prisons are. Rather than rehabilitate inmates, prisons consistently undermine the autonomy of prisoners to such an extent that they emerge from long sentences far less likely to lead rewarding lives of responsible citizenship. I agree that it is asinine to organize a so-called corrective system in such a way as to systematically disable a nonnegligible portion of the population, but (if we assume for the sake of argument that no one is either wrongly punished or overpunished) I am not convinced that it is necessarily impermissible. Put harshly, if you do not want to be confined in psychologically destructive conditions, then do not violate anyone else's rights; and if you do wrong others, you cannot complain about being detained in conditions that impede healthy maturation. Having said that, I do believe that one's rights can be violated by the conditions of one's incarceration. If one had to sleep on a dirt floor because the state was unwilling to pay for beds and linens, for instance, one might have a legitimate complaint. Or imagine that prisoners were literally housed with lions and tigers. In these circumstances, a prisoner might rightfully complain *even if she was guilty and the length of her sentence was not excessive.*

These scenarios might seem ridiculous, but some of the prisons in the United States are so dangerous that I would unquestionably prefer a situation with no beds and linens, and I might even opt to take my chances with lions and tigers. Many maximum security prisons are effectively controlled by violent gangs and/or corrupt guards who prey with impunity on non–gang members. If the state wanted to, it could ensure that inmates are not continually threatened with rape and other forms of violent attack. The sad truth, though, is that we do not care enough to spend the necessary money. As a consequence, we violate the rights of masses of prisoners by knowingly exposing them to unreasonable risks. To clarify: a prisoner who has been raped by a fellow inmate would not necessarily have a legitimate complaint against the state; it would depend upon what measures the state took to protect its prisoners. If the state went to considerable lengths to ensure that almost no one would be subject to attack and yet one inmate assaulted another, then the state would not have violated anyone's rights (even though the attack occurred on its watch, as it were). But if in an attempt to save money the state foreseeably and avoidably detains prisoners in circumstances in which they are highly vulnerable to violent attack, even those lucky enough to avoid abuse will have had their rights violated by having been exposed to unreasonable risks of such horrific harm.

Here a critic might wonder why an especially vicious wrongdoer cannot forfeit her right not to endure these dangerous conditions. After all, given that I am open to the possibility that all rights (even the right to life) can be forfeited, I seem to be in no position to protest that every inmate in a US maximum security prison has a right to better conditions. In response, I concede that some particularly loathsome criminals may well not be wronged by their exposure to such a violent environment, but I do not need to claim that every inmate in the United States' maximum security prisons is being treated unjustly. It is enough if some are. And given how many people are in prison for nonviolent drug crimes, it seems plausible to suppose that masses of people are having their rights violated by being forced to endure an unreasonable risk of terrible harms.

PUNISHING AGAINST A BACKGROUND OF INJUSTICE

Finally, I would like to focus on *who* is being punished, because, as many have noted, US prisons tend to be disproportionately filled with poor minorities. Indeed, although the recent spike in meth use in predominantly white rural communities is changing this, many prison populations are so dark that black inmates refer to their confines as "slave ships that don't move." It is important to be clear that the current racial make-up of our prisons does not automatically show that the system is corrupt, since it is always possible the demographics of the prison population merely reflects the fact that, the darker your skin, the more likely you are to culpably violate the rights of others. But while this is a logical possibility, it is not probable. It is far more plausible to suppose that the racial make-up of our prisons is the result of grave social and economic injustice.

The opportunities for a good life are horribly inequitably distributed within the United States. Indeed, just as I noted at the outset of this chapter that no name-brand theorist defends the status quo regarding punishment, the very same could be said about our current economic state of affairs. We have a horrible history of racial injustice that has never been satisfactorily redressed. Wealthy whites in the United States have segregated our communities, hoarded our advantages, systematically withdrawn funding from black neighborhoods, and—surprise, surprise—some of these disproportionately black neighborhoods are now crippled by severe drug and crime problems. And how have we addressed these problems? By increasing our police surveillance, heightening our prosecution, and enhancing our punishments for denizens of these struggling communities. Rather than invest the funds necessary to improve equality of opportunity, we focus our punitive efforts on those who have relatively few viable legal options. (Indeed, the police presence in the poor ghettos is so dense, intrusive, and militaristic that rap artists—without a hint of irony or the slightest fear of being misunderstood by their listeners—refer to it as the "Occupation.") And one need not engage in conspiracy theory to speculate that the chief reason there has been virtually no effective political backlash against the overcriminalization, overpunishment, and inhumane prison conditions canvassed above is that these rights violations are overwhelmingly perpetrated upon politically marginalized, poor minorities.[7]

What should we make of this? Are the ghetto poor justified in committing crimes? Are they excused? Is the injustice of the economic status quo a mitigating circumstance? In my view, how we answer these questions depends upon what crimes the ghetto poor commit. If poor minorities are protesting the injustice of the existing system, then arguably they are entirely justified in breaking the law. To offer just one striking example: Martin Luther King, Jr., had a right not to be imprisoned in the Birmingham jail for his civil disobedience. It may also be that the ghetto poor are justified or at least (partially) excused for committing some types of economic crime. After all, do not the uncompensated historical injustices along with contemporary racial and class-based injustice call into question the legitimacy of existing property laws and the criminal sanctions that uphold them? To appreciate the force of this point, imagine that someone steals some food from a slave-owner's kitchen. Does it matter whether this food was taken by one of the slave-owner's slaves or by one of her slave-owning neighbors? I presume that it does. Even if the slave is neither justified nor excused in taking what the law proclaims belongs to the slave-owner (and I am not convinced that this is so), surely the injustice of the slave/slave-owner relationship is a mitigating factor.

Rather than press this line here, though, I would merely like to propose two much more modest conclusions. First, even if the US legal system is well within its rights to punish *mala in se* crimes, it may lack authority over the ghetto poor with respect to *mala prohibita* crimes. Second, we should be damn sure that there is no better way to help the ghetto poor than to expand criminalization, increase police surveillance, and enhance punishment.

First, as I emphasized above, one can affirm the state's exclusive right to prosecute and punish rights violators without necessarily believing that states have the moral power to unilaterally make otherwise permissible conduct wrongful merely by prohibiting it. In order to have this latter type of authority over its constituents, presumably a state must at least do a satisfactory job of securing a just peace. But if the current distribution of benefits, burdens, and economic opportunities in the United States is egregiously unjust, then the government that helped establish and continues to prop up this inequitable arrangement would at least seem to lack authority over those who are unjustly disadvantaged. As Tommie Shelby explains, "I would conjecture that in an affluent society with a recent history of overt racial exclusion, no reasonable standard for tolerable injustice is compatible with persistent ghetto conditions. If this conjecture is accurate, then when the ghetto poor in the United States refuse to accept menial jobs or to respect the authority of the law qua law, they do not thereby violate the principle of reciprocity or shirk valid civic obligations."[8] Thus, even if we assume for the sake of argument that the US government has the moral authority to criminalize the self-regarding behavior of affluent white citizens who reside in the segregated suburbs, it may lack the moral standing to criminalize the otherwise permissible behavior of the ghetto poor.

Second, when a government has been complicit in gross injustices that have obviously contributed to the problems currently facing the ghetto poor, it incurs a special, remedial obligation to help solve these problems. It is not *inconceivable* that the most promising way to solve these problems is to increase policing, prosecution, and punishment, but as our experience with the prohibition of alcohol makes plain, this seems (to put it mildly) highly improbable. It seems far more likely that we could do much more good by investing more aggressively in education and preventive healthcare, among other things. As Michelle Alexander notes:

> No one should ever attempt to minimize the harm caused by crack cocaine and the related violence. . . . As a nation, though, we had a choice about how to respond. Some countries faced with rising drug crime or seemingly intractable rates of drug abuse and drug addiction chose the path of drug treatment, prevention, and education or economic investment in crime-ridden communities. Portugal, for example, responded to persistent problems of drug addiction and abuse by decriminalizing the possession of all drugs and redirecting the money that would have been spent putting drug users in cages into drug treatment and prevention. Ten years later, Portugal reported that rates of drug abuse and addiction had plummeted, and drug-related crime was on the decline as well. Numerous paths were available to us as a nation, in the wake of the crack crisis, yet for reasons traceable largely to racial politics and fear mongering we chose war.[9]

It may (or may not) be that pursuing Portugal's less punitive approach would be more expensive, but given our collective role in creating the existing problems, the state is obligated to play its part in the solution. To emphasize: given our responsibility for the status quo, we are in no position to object to the costs of pursuing alternative solutions. If all of this is correct, then we should regard the preponderance of poor minorities in our prisons as a compelling sign that we as a society are adding insult (and considerably more injury!) to the initial injuries sustained as a result of our collective failure to achieve even a minimal level of social justice.

A PROVOCATIVE ANALOGY

Imagine that a dictator orders her secret police to round up a hundred citizens a day. Some of those who are seized are wrongdoers, some are political opponents, and some are merely innocent people to be raped by the dictator and/or her family and friends. I assume without argument that third parties would be justified in forcibly interfering with these officials as they attempt to collect these citizens for the dictator. Indeed, given the magnitude and number of rights violations at stake, I should think that there would be nothing disproportionate about using violence, if necessary, against the dictator's soldiers. Admittedly, one could not disable these officials without helping some wrongdoers avoid punishment, but if there is any truth to the old adage that it is better to let ten guilty people go free than to wrongly punish one innocent person, this fact would not necessarily render one's resistance impermissible. But notice: if I am right that the US criminal legal system routinely (1) punishes innocent people, (2) overpunishes guilty folks, (3) incarcerates inmates under inhumane conditions where they are exposed to unreasonable risks of rape and other forms of violent attack, and (4) does all of this against a background of systemic social and economic injustice, then why should we not endorse the same position with respect to those who work in the US criminal legal institution? Why may we not storm the prisons and use (proportionate) force against the prison guards in defense of those who are being wrongly punished, overpunished, or held in inhumane conditions?

In response to this question, it is tempting to object that my comparison is obviously unfair; even if far more than one hundred people are daily having their human rights violated by the US criminal legal system, these rights violations are merely the inadvertent collateral damage of a democratic system, not the intended consequences of a malicious tyrant. As I see it, however, neither the appeal to democracy nor the difference in intentions renders this thought experiment inapt.

The importance of the United States' being a democracy can be questioned either factually or morally. Factually, one might object that, while the United States calls itself a democracy, it is in fact much more of a plutocracy, insofar as money has an enormous impact upon how laws are made and enforced. Even if the United States had unassailable democratic credentials, however, this would not necessarily justify the status quo, because some institutions are so objectionable that they cannot be sanitized by even an impeccable democratic pedigree. Imagine that the United States democratically decided to reinstitute slavery, for instance. The fact that a majority democratically chose to enslave a minority would do nothing to justify such an abhorrent practice, nor would it give external parties a principled reason to refrain from forcibly intervening. So, just as a country like Norway would not have to refrain from interfering in a democratic United States if doing so was necessary to dismantle the latter's institution of slavery, the United States' status as a democracy does not imply that Norway may not forcibly interfere with the US criminal legal system.

What about the fact that no one responsible for the US criminal legal system exhibits any malice toward those who are wrongly punished, overpunished, or held in unconscionable conditions? To begin, we must concede that there are contexts in which intentions are paramount. If we are trying to determine the culpability of a leader, for instance, it matters enormously whether we are appraising a tyrant who knowingly rounds up innocent victims to rape or a queen who (on the basis of her most trusted advisors) arrests folks for wearing blue shirts on Tuesdays because she genuinely believes that dressing in this fashion will invite the wrath of vengeful gods. It is important to stress, though, that rather than trying to decide whether or how to punish the leader, we want to know whether defensive force against a rights-violating regime is justified. And because our principal concern is to rescue imperiled citizens, the intention of the lawmakers is irrelevant. Notice, for instance, that I am no less entitled to forcibly interfere with a doctor's potentially fatal treatment of an unconscious patient merely because this physician genuinely believes that this treatment is necessary to cure the patient. Given this, it appears that both US citizens and foreign parties would be just as entitled to forcibly interfere with US criminal legal officials as they would be to oppose our hypothetical dictator's secret police.

CONCLUSION

The particular brand of forfeiture theory I espouse includes a number of relatively controversial claims, including that (1) every right can be forfeited, (2) once the right against punishment has been forfeited, hard treatment becomes permissible even if it serves no purpose, and (3) there is no general moral right not to be punished until one's guilt has been established via a fair and reliable procedure. Given these normative building blocks, my view would seem maximally permissive of a wide variety of criminal legal systems. Even so, my approach cannot justify anything like the status quo. On the contrary, once we look at the US criminal legal system through the lens of moral side constraints rather than in terms of general justifying aims, it becomes clear that we are not merely doing a poor job of achieving valuable goods, we are violating basic moral rights on a massive scale. Indeed, as the preceding discussion illustrates, it is no exaggeration to say that the status quo constitutes a widespread and systematic human rights atrocity.

NOTES

Chapter 1

1. David Dolinko, "Some Thoughts about Retributivism," *Ethics* 101 (1991): 539, puts this distinction between why we might *want* to punish and why we may *permissibly* punish in terms of rational versus moral justification.
2. Douglas Husak, "Does the State Have a Monopoly to Punish Crime?," in Chad Flanders and Zachary Hoskins (eds.), *The New Philosophy of Criminal Law* (London: Rowman and Littlefield, 2016), 98. The stigmatizing nature of punishment was first emphasized by Joel Feinberg in his landmark essay "The Expressive Function of Punishment," reprinted in Feinberg, *Doing and Deserving* (Princeton: Princeton University Press, 1970), 95–118.
3. W. D. Ross, *The Right and the Good* (Oxford: Oxford University Press, 1930), 60–61.
4. It is a slight oversimplification to say that forfeiture is necessary and sufficient for punishment to be permissible. First, given that I am not an absolutist about rights, forfeiture is not, strictly speaking, necessary. If one could prevent a nuclear holocaust only by punishing an innocent person, for instance, then presumably one may do so. And forfeiture is not always sufficient to make punishment permissible, because there may be other factors that ground obligations. If Alison promises Betty that she will not punish Carol, for instance, then the fact that Carol has forfeited her right not to be punished is not sufficient to make it permissible for Alison to punish her. So my claim that rights forfeiture is necessary and sufficient should be understood as the view that (1) *in the absence of extraordinary circumstances*, it is impermissible to punish someone who has not forfeited her rights, and (2) if someone has forfeited her right not to be

punished, then one may permissibly punish her even if doing so is not necessary to promote some important aim.

5. My insistence that all rights may be enforced appears to conflict with Jeremy Waldron's famous claim that there is "a right to do wrong," but I suspect that our differences are merely terminological. To motivate the idea that there is a right to do wrong, Waldron begins with a series of cases in which we may not interfere with an agent even though she acts wrongly. It is important to recognize, though, that none of these cases (in my view, at least) involves a rights violation. Rather, they are examples (such as refusing "to give a stranger on the street the time of day when he asks for it") of non-rights-violating behavior that reflects poorly on the agent's character. Jeremy Waldron, "A Right to Do Wrong," *Ethics* 92 (1981): 21.
6. Following Julia Driver, "The Suberogatory," *Australasian Journal of Philosophy* 70 (1992): 286–295, and Michael Zimmerman, *The Concept of Moral Obligation* (Cambridge: Cambridge University Press, 1996), I understand a suberogatory act to be a permissible action that nonetheless reflects poorly on the agent's character (and thus an omission would be suberogatory if action is not morally required but inaction nonetheless reflects poorly on the agent's character). The term "suberogatory" may not be used that widely, but the category it designates is a common one. One canonical case in the literature, for instance, is Judith Jarvis Thomson's example of a woman whom Thomson labels "indecent" because she seeks an abortion in her seventh month of pregnancy "just to avoid the nuisance of postponing a trip abroad." Thomson, "A Defense of Abortion," *Philosophy & Public Affairs* 1 (1971): 65.
7. Jeffrie G. Murphy, "Blackmail: A Preliminary Inquiry," *Monist* 63 (1980): 168 n. 6.
8. Joel Feinberg, "The Nature and Value of Rights," reprinted in *Rights, Justice, and the Bounds of Liberty* (Princeton: Princeton University Press, 1980), 143–155.
9. Alec Walen, "Retributive Justice," in Edward N. Zalta (ed.), *The Stanford Encyclopedia of Philosophy* (summer 2015 ed.), http://plato.stanford.edu/archives/sum2015/entries/justice-retributive/.

Chapter 2

1. As much as Tadros condemns retributivists for mistakenly (he thinks) believing that some impersonal value is achieved through punishment, he thinks strong forfeiture theory is even more implausible for alleging that we may permissibly punish even if doing so would achieve no good whatsoever.
2. For a thorough examination of whether the offense taken by others can give rise to a duty to modify one's behavior, see Joel Feinberg's *Offense to Others* (New York: Oxford University Press, 1985).

3. Given the extreme acts to which Brandes consented, it is natural to wonder whether he was of sound mind. I acknowledge that it might have been permissible for a third party to forcibly interfere in order to psychologically examine Brandes, but I am not convinced that we are entitled to pronounce that Brandes was necessarily incompetent merely because he had such unusual sexual tastes and preferences.
4. As Jeff McMahan writes: "Consent to be killed is not sufficient on its own to make killing permissible. In cases in which a person is not liable to be killed, and killing that person is not justified as the lesser evil, consent seems to be a necessary but not sufficient condition of the permissibility of killing. It contributes to the justification for killing but only in the presence of another good reason for killing, such as that the person's life has ceased to be worth living." *Killing in War* (Oxford: Oxford University Press, 2009), 56.
5. See Victor Tadros, "Consent to Harm," *Current Legal Problems* 64 (2011): 23–49.
6. Thomas E. Hill, Jr., "Self-regarding Suicide," in Thomas E. Hill (ed.), *Autonomy and Self-Respect* (Cambridge: Cambridge University Press, 1991), 95. And later Hill stresses that "the principle expresses an ideal rather than a duty. Thus questions of blame, censure, and enforcement associated with violations of duty are not at issue here" (95).
7. To offer just one common example, notice how much emphasis parents place on teaching their young children to share their toys, even though few believe that the other children on the playground have a *right* to play with their child's toys.
8. On the idea of rights talk being the language of conflict adjudication, see Carl Wellman, *A Theory of Rights* (Totowa, NJ: Rowman and Allanheld, 1985), 96–102.
9. I should acknowledge that nonidentity cases provide a potential exception to my claim that all duties are owed to a second, specific individual. Because nonidentity cases are sui generis (and because I am open to the idea that one may permissibly be punished for violating a duty in a nonidentity case), I will not explore this potential exception further.
10. *Anarchy, State and Utopia* (New York: Basic Books, 1974), 138. Interestingly, Nozick does not allege that these sadists would act impermissibly.
11. I say "at most" here because, as Eric Mack reminded me, there is a long tradition—in which John Locke is conspicuous—of theorists who believe that one can forfeit one's right to life even though one cannot alienate it. Thus, even if I am wrong about our ability to waive certain rights, this may have *no* implications for forfeiture.
12. An alternative way to capture this idea would be to insist that mere forfeiture is not enough to make punishment permissible; in addition to forfeiture, the punishment must be necessary to secure some good.

13. McMahan, *Killing in War*, 8–9.
14. As McMahan explains in *Killing in War* (8), "I draw the distinction between liability to harm and desert of harm by reference to the further distinction between the instrumental and the noninstrumental. Desert is noninstrumental. If a person deserves to be harmed, there is a moral reason for harming him that is independent of the further consequences of harming him. Giving him what he deserves is an end in itself. Although a deserved harm is bad for the person who suffers it, it is, from an impersonal point of view, intrinsically *good*. By contrast, a person is liable to be harmed only if harming him will serve some further purpose."
15. For instructive surveys of the putative problems with forfeiture theory, see Richard L. Lippke, "Criminal Offenders and Right Forfeiture," *Journal of Social Philosophy* 32 (2001): 78–89, and David Boonin, *The Problem of Punishment* (New York: Cambridge University Press, 2008), 103–119. One additional potential objection, the "problem of relatedness," is treated separately in chapter 6.
16. Alan Goldman, "The Paradox of Punishment," *Philosophy & Public Affairs* 9 (1979): 42–58, Christopher Morris, "Punishment and Loss of Moral Standing," *Canadian Journal of Philosophy* 21 (1991): 53–79, and John Simmons, "Locke and the Right to Punish," *Philosophy & Public Affairs* 20 (1991): 311–349.
17. Boonin, *Problem of Punishment*, 107–108.
18. I have no quarrel with forfeiture theorists who arrive at the view via these other premises; it is just that I am reluctant to base my account on any of these particular arguments.
19. Victor Tadros, *The Ends of Harm* (Oxford: Oxford University Press, 2011).
20. For arguments that Tadros's account fails on its own terms, see Kimberly Kessler Ferzan, "Rethinking *The Ends of Harm*," *Law and Philosophy* 32 (2013): 177–198.
21. Indeed, even critics like David Boonin, who list any number of objections, concede that this is a plausible premise.
22. If only the victim has a right to punish, then perhaps vigilantism does not constitute such a problem. There are two worries about this potential response, though. First, the dominant view (to which I subscribe) is that, while the victim enjoys a special claim to reparation, all enjoy a competitive right to punish. And second, even if we assume that the victim has an exclusive executive right, we still need a plausible story about how this right gets transferred from the victim to the state. In theory, individuals could transfer this right to the state via a social contract. As virtually everyone now concedes, however, contemporary states have not in fact garnered the morally valid consent of all of their constituents.
23. John Simmons observes as much in "Locke and the Right to Punish," 311. As he puts it: "There is, however, a fourth way of understanding the question,

which is not so often touched on in the literature on punishment because it places the question more squarely within the province of political philosophy."

24. A standard move here (which seems equally available to a rights forfeiture theorist) is to suggest an "equivalence" approach that allows authorities to punish criminals in ways that are distinct from, but equivalent to, rape, torture, and such. Against this approach, Boonin has recently countered that "if a given right really is equivalent to another, then if it is unacceptable to deprive someone of one right, it must be equally unacceptable to deprive him of the other" (*Problem of Punishment*, 111).
25. As Michael Moore emphasizes in *Placing Blame* (Oxford: Oxford University Press, 1997), 88: "It is quite possible to be a retributivist and to be against both the death penalty and *lex talionis*, the idea that crimes should be punished by like acts being done to the criminal."
26. Perhaps the most obvious reason to eschew *lex talionis* (and its rights forfeiture analogue) is that it appears entirely insensitive to the various degrees of culpability. Insofar as one focuses exclusively on the harm done (or the right transgressed), one would recommend the same punishments for intentional, reckless, and negligent agents.
27. Daniel McDermott, "The Permissibility of Punishment," *Law and Philosophy* 20 (2001): 425.
28. Boonin, *Problem of Punishment*, 115–117.
29. David Luban, "Fairness to Rightness: Jurisdiction, Legality, and the Legitimacy of International Criminal Law," in Samantha Besson and John Tasioulas (eds.), *The Philosophy of International Law* (Oxford: Oxford University Press, 2010), 584.
30. Luban, "Fairness to Rightness," 584. For an explanation as to why the punishments at Nuremberg may have been justified even if their ex post facto nature rendered them unjust, see Andrew Altman and Christopher Heath Wellman, "A Defense of International Criminal Law," *Ethics* 115 (2004): 35–67.
31. Doug Husak, "The De Minimis 'Defence' to Criminal Liability," in R. A. Duff and Stuart Green (eds.), *Philosophical Foundations of Criminal Law* (Oxford: Oxford University Press, 2011), 328–351.

Chapter 3

1. See Robert Nozick, *Anarchy, State and Utopia* (New York: Basic Books, 1974), Murray Rothbard, *The Ethics of Liberty* (Atlantic Highlands, NJ: Humanities Press, 1982), and John Simmons, "Locke and the Right to Punish," *Philosophy & Public Affairs* 20 (1991): 311–349.
2. Although I will consistently refer only to deterrence, I should stress that the state both deters *and coordinates*. Many of us do not need to be deterred from

wronging others, we just need a clear account of what the rules are. Insofar as the state is best positioned to definitely establish a single set of rules for all, it provides a vital coordinating function.

3. Here a critic might object that, although states may be more effective than individuals at realizing the aims of a system of punishment, it is a false dichotomy to compare only these two options. Many believe that competing private protective agencies could do a better job than a state monopoly, for instance. I defend the preferability of the state elsewhere and will not retrace those arguments here. For now, I shall merely acknowledge that a fully adequate defense of state punishment must show (among other things) that no less coercive option exists.
4. In my view, it is also essential that the state provide these vital benefits for everyone without imposing unreasonable burdens upon any of us. If a state could secure the aims of punishment only by enslaving all of its constituents, for instance, then it would not be justified in doing so.
5. Insofar as my account of legitimacy focuses upon a state's ability and willingness to perform the requisite political functions (rather than its having garnered the consent of its constituents), one might worry that my approach amounts to an unargued privileging of the political status quo and an implicit dismissal of the many kinds of *historical* facts that seem paradigmatically to *legitimate* the claims groups make on behalf of their right to control the state. While my account is clearly functional rather than historical in the first instance, it need not be insensitive to all historical considerations. To see why, imagine that New Zealand is satisfactorily realizing the important aims of punishment and thus is (on my account) legitimate. If Australia then forcibly annexed New Zealand, it would thereby wrongly fail to respect the political self-determination to which New Zealand is entitled as a legitimate state. Most important, notice that my view does not commit me to the view that Australia's jurisdiction over New Zealand's territory would become legitimate as soon as it were adequately securing the aims of the punitive process, because there is nothing that prohibits me from objecting to Australia's objectionable disrespect for New Zealand's sovereign rights. For more on the self-determination to which legitimate states are entitled, see my "Group Autonomy and State Sovereignty," in *Liberal Rights and Responsibilities* (New York: Oxford University Press, 2014), 145–169.
6. I should add that, while states may tax their constituents to fund the institution of punishment, it does not follow that they may permissibly tax citizens to fund whatever tasks they assign themselves. There may be other things that would justify taxes, but they would have to pass the same type of tests that I have argued the institution of punishment does. In particular, a state may not assign itself a task unless (1) the state is able and willing to secure the goods in question, (2) these goods cannot be satisfactorily secured through any other, noncoercive route, and (3) these goods are sufficiently important to justify the

coercion involved in the state's imposition. Obviously, many things that existing states do fail to satisfy at least one of these three conditions.

7. I explain and defend the samaritan theory of political legitimacy in "Liberalism, Samaritanism, and Political Legitimacy," *Philosophy and Public Affairs* 25 (1996): 211–237.
8. Because I eschew absolutism, I cannot rule out the possibility that samaritanism would justify punishing the innocent in extreme cases. Patrick Tomlin has a nice discussion of samaritanism and punishment (and the problems this issue creates for Victor Tadros's duty view of punishment) in his excellent essay "Innocence Lost: A Problem for Punishment as Duty" (forthcoming in *Law and Philosophy*).
9. Nozick presumably had no interest in international criminal law, but he seemed to realize this basic point when he wrote (*Anarchy, State and Utopia*, 137): "Is the general right to punish so counterintuitive? If some great wrong were committed in another country which refuses to punish it (perhaps the government is in league with, or is itself, the wrongdoer), wouldn't it be all right for you to punish the wrongdoer, to inflict some harm on him for his act?"
10. Mary Robinson, foreword to *The Princeton Principles on Universal Jurisdiction* (2001), http://lapa.princeton.edu/hosteddocs/unive_jur.pdf.
11. Geoffrey Robertson, *Crimes against Humanity* (London: Allen Lane, 1999), 375. It is worth noting that this prevailing view is not restricted to international lawyers. Larry May, who has provided an exceptionally extensive and sophisticated philosophical analysis of crimes against humanity, is representative of philosophers who have worked on this topic. As May puts it: "In domestic settings, criminal prosecutions should only go forward when group-based individual harm is alleged—that is, harm that affects not only the individual victim but also the community. . . . In international criminal law, harms that are prosecuted should similarly affect a public—what could be called the world community, or humanity." As a consequence, May proposes what he labels "the international harm principle," according to which international society may prosecute and punish only those crimes which harm all of humanity. See May, *Crimes against Humanity: A Normative Account* (Cambridge: Cambridge University Press, 2005), 80 and 82.
12. Many who use the term seem to mean "crimes that are particularly atrocious or 'inhumane.'" Often this is because they (wrongly) presume that the conscience-shocking character of the crimes explains why all of humanity is thereby harmed. In other cases, however, people apparently conceive of crimes against humanity as being particularly atrocious *rather than* as harming all of humanity. There are two things to notice about this alternate understanding of crimes against humanity. First, for the vast bulk of international lawyers who adopt a Westphalian perspective, this conception of crimes against humanity would not "provide the key to unlock the closed door of state sovereignty."

Second and related, even if we reject the Westphalian outlook, it is not clear why the international community is entitled to prosecute and punish all and only those criminals whose acts are especially inhumane.

13. Andrew Altman and I explain and defend this alternative understanding of international criminal law in our book, *A Liberal Theory of International Justice* (New York: Oxford University Press, 2009). There we also explain why a legitimate state A has a right that external bodies, such as state B, not interfere with the criminal prosecution and punishment of criminals in A, *even if B could do a better job*. In our view, legitimate states are entitled to self-determination as long as they adequately perform the requisite political functions of protecting the human rights of their constituents and respecting the rights of all others. If so, legitimate states enjoy a privileged position of dominion even against others who might do a better job. An instructive analogy here is parental authority. If my wife and I are doing a satisfactory job of raising our children, for instance, then others may not forcibly take our children from us and raise them, even if they would be better parents. Similarly, if the United States is satisfactorily performing the requisite political functions, then Canada would have no right to unilaterally assign itself the task of punishing criminals in Detroit, for example, even if Canada could do so better than the United States currently does.

Chapter 4

1. R. A. Duff, *Answering for Crime* (Oxford: Hart, 2007), 52.
2. Duff, *Answering for Crime*, 144.
3. R. A. Duff, "Torts, Crimes and Vindication: Whose Wrong Is It?," in Matthew Dyson (ed.), *Unravelling Tort and Crime* (Cambridge: Cambridge University Press, 2014), 173.
4. R. A. Duff, "Towards a Modest Legal Moralism," *Criminal Law and Philosophy* 8 (2014): 232–233.
5. Joel Feinberg, "Voluntary Euthanasia and the Inalienable Right to Life," *Philosophy & Public Affairs* 7 (1978): 102.
6. Judith Jarvis Thomson introduces the distinction between infringements and violations in "Self-defense and Rights," reprinted in *Rights, Restitution and Risk* (Cambridge, MA: Harvard University Press, 1986), 40.
7. John Oberdiek, "Lost in Moral Space: On the Infringement/Violating Distinction and Its Place in the Theory of Rights," *Law and Philosophy* 23 (2004): 334–345.
8. Nancy Davis, "Rights, Permission and Compensation," *Philosophy & Public Affairs* 14 (1985): 382, argues along these lines in response to Phillip Montague (who has voiced the same type of concern as Oberdiek). As Davis puts it, "both the person who regretfully causes harm and the person

who willfully inflicts it may be obliged to compensate a victim for his or her loss (even though the first acts permissibly while the second does not). But the vandal's debt does not end there. The vandal is rightly punished for the destructive act, rightly required to pay a penalty as well as compensation."

9. Given that they have not acted impermissibly, one might question whether rights infringers like Feinberg's stranded backpacker may permissibly be forced to compensate the person whose right they infringe. I believe that, just as we say that divorce may be permissible on the condition that one pays alimony and continues to contribute one's fair share toward raising the children, the proper description of the moral relations in Feinberg's case is to say that the backpacker may permissibly enter the cabin and consume the owner's food *as long as she subsequently compensates the owner*. Thus, entry and consumption followed by compensation is permissible, whereas entry and consumption without compensation is impermissible. If so, just like a divorcee who pays her fair share of alimony and child support, a stranded backpacker who adequately compensates the cabin owner after entering and consuming is neither civilly nor criminally liable. But a backpacker who refuses to compensate the owner after entering and consuming has harmed the owner and acted impermissibly, and thus (like a divorcee who has failed to pay her alimony and/or child support) may be held civilly and criminally liable.
10. My sharp distinction between deplorable and culpable (which I explained in the introduction) entails that, for me, all culpability is rights-related. That is, one cannot be culpable without at least attempting to violate a right.
11. James Edwards has noted that my account of tort law as an appropriate response to rights-related harms does not square well with the fact that most legal systems include apparently harmless torts like libel and trespass. Following a helpful suggestion from John Oberdiek, I am inclined to adopt Joel Feinberg's account of harm (from *Harm to Others*) as a setback to interests. And given the plausibility of supposing that we have interests in things such as our reputation and exclusive dominion over our real property, it seems appropriate to conclude that libel and trespass are in fact harmful. If there are acts that are harmless even according to this capacious notion of harm, then there would be no victim who needs to be made whole, and thus no need for a tort remedy.
12. Victor Tadros, *The Ends of Harm* (Oxford: Oxford University Press, 2011), 278–279, offers an explanation as to why there may be practical, but no principled, distinction between civil and criminal wrongs.
13. Douglas Husak, "The De Minimis 'Defence' to Criminal Liability," in R. A. Duff and Stuart Green (eds.), *Philosophical Foundations of Criminal Law* (Oxford: Oxford University Press, 2011), 350.
14. As Patrick Tomlin has pointed out to me, my view may be compatible with at least some (of what I would call "hybrid") strict liability offenses. Having a

strict liability offense of murder if one kills someone in the course of committing a felony may be an example. This offense involves strict liability because it automatically applies whenever one kills someone, but it is hybrid insofar as it applies only if one is committing a felony. (I would regard it as unjust to apply this strict liability offense to anyone who was nonculpably committing a felony.)

15. Indeed, in many instances (including cases of domestic abuse), fear of the defendant retaliating may lead victims to worry that they would be *less* safe after prosecution.
16. Randy E. Barnett, "Restitution: A New Paradigm of Criminal Justice," *Ethics* 87 (1977): 287–288.
17. David Boonin, who is sympathetic to Barnett's thesis, lists and responds to these objections in chapter 5 of *The Problem of Punishment* (New York: Cambridge University Press, 2008).
18. Franklin G. Miller, "Restitution and Punishment: A Reply to Barnett," *Ethics* 88 (1978): 359.
19. Tadros, *Ends of Harm*, 99.
20. Roger Pilon, "Criminal Remedies: Restitution, Punishment, or Both?," *Ethics* 88 (1978): 351.
21. As Tadros explains (*Ends of Harm*, 83), "but the criminal justice system is very expensive. It uses considerable resources, and hence labour power, of citizens to maintain and operate it. Retributivists need to show that citizens may be forced to contribute to its maintenance and operation, and simply showing that the suffering of wrongdoers is good provides only a modest component of that case."
22. Retributivists who resist this conclusion should ask themselves whether they would support taxation in order to create and sustain a comparable system designed solely to reward the virtuous. If retributivism is about giving agents what they deserve, then it seems equally concerned with punishing wrongdoers and rewarding the virtuous. Thus, once we disentangle retributivism from deterrence, consistency would seem to require those who endorse taxation in order to punish the guilty also to support taxing everyone in order to support a state system that rewards the virtuous. As David Dolinko notes in "Some Thoughts about Retributivism," *Ethics* 101 (1991): 542, "the government, state, or 'society' does not automatically take it upon itself to give people what they deserve in other respects. People, for example, who do good deeds—people who are kind, charitable, caring, who take care of their relatives or help strangers in distress—might be thought to deserve reward, yet the state does not routinely administer such a reward system."
23. As Tadros puts it (*Ends of Harm*, 285), "the justification of general deterrence is, I believe, crucial to justifying state punishment. It is crucial in that it is the only thing that could plausibly justify using significant state resources to

develop and maintain the kind of criminal justice institutions that are necessary for the maintenance of civil society."

24. Boonin, for instance, embraces Barnett's conclusion at least in part because he believes that civil law can provide a sufficient deterrent against wrongdoing. *Problem of Punishment*, 264–267.
25. Alternatively, one might think that in the transition from the state of nature to a legitimate state individuals gain the advantage of greater security but lose both the right to engage in vigilante justice and the right to have the state punish those who wrong one.
26. The arguments social contract theorists traditionally offer in defense of the state's monopoly over the criminal legal system would seem to apply equally to tort law. Indeed, given that individuals are typically more concerned to receive (what they regard as) fair monetary compensation than they are that the perpetrator is punished, we should be even more worried about "vigilante compensation" than vigilante justice. If so, we seem to need governmental control over criminal and civil proceedings. But given our conclusion that criminal law can be defended only on contingent empirical grounds, it is worth asking whether a state might permissibly have only criminal law. Would anyone's rights necessarily be violated by getting rid of the tort system?

    Even if redirecting the resources we currently expend on tort law to criminal law meant that we would have dramatically fewer crimes, we would still worry about both (1) the rights to compensation for the remaining few who have their rights violated, and (2) the rights to restitution of those who have their rights infringed. Because rights to restitution are defeasible, I cannot rule out that there may be compelling reasons that would override these rights, but it strikes me that the right to restitution is weightier than either the right to personally punish or the more general right to see that one's right violator is punished. To see this, imagine that Tom burns down Jerry's house. It seems a much more serious deprivation to say that Jerry may not collect damages from Tom than it does to say either that Jerry may not punish Tom or that he may not see that Tom is punished. So, while I cannot summarily rule out the permissibility of a legitimate state permissibly abandoning tort law, I am skeptical that there would be real-world cases analogous to the Truth and Reconciliation Commission in which it would be justified.

Chapter 5

1. More precisely, I should say that there are no general, moral, judicial, procedural rights. The various components of this more cumbersome description will be explained below.

2. Many theorists (especially those working in the Kantian, Hobbesian, and Hegelian traditions) incorporate the existence of procedural rights into their very definitions of punishment. John Rawls in "Two Concepts of Rules," in Samuel Freeman (ed.), *John Rawls: Collected Papers* (Cambridge, MA: Harvard University Press, 2001), 26, for instance, specifies that "a person is said to suffer punishment whenever he is legally deprived of some of the normal rights of a citizen on the grounds that he has violated a rule of law, the violation having been established by trial according to due process."
3. Given that no one seriously believes that this person is guilty, one might question whether this condemnation and hard treatment actually constitutes punishment. This is a reasonable question, but my view is that a person who has been framed by a corrupt authority makes perfect sense when she complains of being wrongly punished. And if this is correct, then punishment does not require that those who impose the hard treatment necessarily believe that the defendant is actually guilty. I am grateful to Antony Duff for raising this potential concern.
4. Those who hold that one's rights cannot be violated unless one is harmed will be skeptical of this claim. If one believes that risk is a purely subjective matter, for instance, then one might deny that A wrongs B when A engages in (what from A's perspective) appears to be risky behavior that does not result in harm to B. See Larry Alexander, "Are Procedural Rights Derivative Substantive Rights?," *Law and Philosophy* 17 (1998): 19–42. I would like to be maximally concessive to defenders of procedural rights, though, so I shall argue that Sandra's rights are not necessarily violated even if we presume that each of us enjoys a right against being exposed to unreasonable risks.
5. I am indebted to Carl Wellman for raising this issue.
6. In fairness to Nozick, I should note that he has several other (extremely original and sophisticated) arguments regarding procedural rights that I do not review here, in part because (as he acknowledges; *Anarchy, State and Utopia* [New York: Basic Books, 1974], 103) some of these arguments merely *assume* the existence of procedural rights, but also because the criticisms I offer below of R. A. Duff's arguments apply equally, mutatis mutandis, to Nozick.
7. R. A. Duff, *Trials and Punishments* (Cambridge: Cambridge University Press, 1986), 114.
8. Duff, *Trials and Punishments*, 113.
9. Another way to characterize this distinction—which I owe to Larry Alexander—is to say that permissibility turns on the facts, whereas culpability depends on the agent's beliefs. Either way, I should acknowledge that my preference for objectivism about moral obligation is far from uncontested. Indeed, since Frank Jackson's landmark article, "Decision-theoretic Consequentialism and the Nearest and Dearest Objection," an enormous literature has been produced with name-brand philosophers lining up on both sides. Notable

recent defenses of objectivism include Frances Kamm, *Intricate Ethics: Rights, Responsibilities, and Permissible Harm* (Oxford: Oxford University Press, 2007), Peter A. Graham, "In Defense of Objectivism about Moral Obligation," *Ethics* 101 (1991): 461–482, and Julia Driver, *Consequentialism* (New York: Routledge, 2012). For sophisticated objections to this view, see Victor Tadros's wonderful discussion of these issues in *The Ends of Harm* (Oxford: Oxford University Press, 2011). In part because it would take me too far afield from the topic of punishment, but also because (as I shall show in chapter 6) embracing objectivism makes the case for rights forfeiture *more* difficult, I feel comfortable helping myself to objectivism with relatively little argument.

10. Duff, *Trials and Punishments*, 112–113. (It is not clear that Duff and I endorse identical positions here because, whereas he claims that the court acts *wrongly*, I suggest that it acts *culpably*.) Nozick comes to a similar conclusion: "It is true that an unreliable procedure will too often find an innocent person guilty. But does applying an unreliable procedure to a *guilty* person violate any right of his? May he, in self-defense, resist the imposition of such a procedure upon himself? But what would he be defending himself against? Too high a probability of a punishment he deserves?" (*Anarchy, State, and Utopia*, 103).
11. Duff, *Trials and Punishments*, 115.
12. One might object that Elizabeth not only acts culpably, she acts impermissibly. As John Simmons insists in "Locke and the Right to Punish," *Philosophy & Public Affairs* 20 (1991): 340, "if I take property from someone who, completely unbeknownst to me, had previously stolen my property, my taking is still theft (and morally impermissible)—even though the property I took from him I might have been entitled to take, if I had taken it *as reparation*." Against this objection, and in defense of the claim that Elizabeth's rights are not violated, notice how awkward it would be to suggest that an informed third party might permissibly interfere with Philippa's actions. After all, what would this third party say to Philippa to justify this interference—"You are in fact entitled to the $20 you are taking, but I will stop you from reclaiming it because you *believe* it belongs to Elizabeth"?
13. Perhaps most notably, Thomas Christiano invokes publicity in his egalitarian defense of democracy in his impressive book *The Constitution of Equality* (Oxford: Oxford University Press, 2008). Christiano argues that equality requires democracy because one is not fully treated as an equal unless one is publicly treated as an equal. And since only democracy publicly treats all citizens as equals, it alone satisfies the requirement that all citizens be treated as equals. (Not surprisingly, my reaction to Christiano's argument parallels my response to Duff's: I agree that it is preferable to be publicly treated as an equal, but I am not convinced that one is not fully equal unless one is publicly equal.

I agree that publicity and equality are both good things, but, contra Christiano, I am inclined to insist that they are distinct things.)

14. Duff, *Trials and Punishments*, 117.
15. Duff, *Trials and Punishments*, 119.
16. Malcolm Gladwell, *Blink* (New York: Back Bay Books, 2007), 276.
17. I am grateful to Ron Mallon for suggesting this possible response.
18. H. L. A. Hart, "Prolegomenon to the Principles of Punishment," reprinted in *Punishment and Responsibility* (Oxford: Clarendon Press, 1968), 5. As I will argue in the next chapter, it is not clear to me that a wrongdoer cannot punish herself, but I do follow Hart in believing that punishment must be "intentionally administered by human beings."
19. Tadros, *Ends of Harm*, 308–309.
20. Allen Buchanan, *The Heart of Human Rights* (New York: Oxford University Press, 2013), 17.
21. Buchanan, *Heart of Human Rights*, 43.
22. James W. Nickel, *Making Sense of Human Rights*, 2nd ed. (Malden, MA: Wiley-Blackwell, 2007), 70.
23. Henry Shue, *Basic Rights*, 2nd ed. (Princeton: Princeton University Press, 1996), 17.
24. Nickel, *Making Sense of Human Rights*, 106.

Chapter 6

1. Warren Quinn, "The Right to Threaten and the Right to Punish," *Philosophy & Public Affairs*, 14 (1985): 322.
2. Richard Lippke, "Criminal Offenders and Right Forfeiture," *Journal of Social Philosophy* 32 (2001): 79.
3. John Simmons, "Locke and the Right to Punish," *Philosophy & Public Affairs* 20 (1991): 339.
4. Jeff McMahan, *Killing in War* (Oxford: Oxford University Press, 2009), 10 (emphasis in original).
5. Stephen Kershnar, "The Structure of Rights Forfeiture in the Context of Culpable Wrongdoing," *Philosophia* 29 (2002): 77. It should be noted that Kershnar prefers the unlimited-reasons approach. Christopher Morris does as well in "Punishment and Loss of Moral Standing," *Canadian Journal of Philosophy* 21 (1991): 77.
6. Andrew Altman and I defend the permissibility of assassination in "From Humanitarian Intervention to Assassination: Human Rights and Political Violence," *Ethics* 118 (2008): 228–257.
7. I infer McMahan's position not merely from the quote above, but also from personal correspondence and conversation with him on this issue.

8. Frances Kamm, *Ethics for Enemies* (Oxford: Oxford University Press, 2011), 79.
9. Simmons, "Locke and the Right to Punish," 340.
10. Simmons, "Locke and the Right to Punish," 340.
11. Simmons, "Locke and the Right to Punish," 340–341.
12. Larry Alexander and Kimberly Ferzan do not adopt my expression of "rights-related culpability," but my view seems compatible with the theory of attempts they defend in *Crime and Culpability: A Theory of Criminal Law* (New York: Cambridge University Press, 2009).
13. To clarify, there may ultimately be no difference in the fairness of my and Simmons's theories, because our two differences may simply cancel one another out. It would initially appear that Simmons restricts the set of people who are morally vulnerable to punishment more narrowly than I, because he insists that one forfeits one's right against punishment only if one violates another's right. This initial appearance is misleading, though, because Simmons adopts a more expansive understanding of rights violations than I. Thus, even though Simmons denies that one may permissibly be punished merely because one *attempted* to violate a right, his limited-reasons approach leads him to categorize acts that I regard to be mere attempts as actual rights violations. And if we ultimately converge on who is morally vulnerable to punishment, Simmons clearly cannot allege that fairness uniquely recommends the limited-reasons approach.
14. Simmons, "Locke and the Right to Punish," 341.
15. For a recent defense of corporal punishment, see Kevin J. Murtagh, "Is Corporally Punishing Criminals Degrading?," *Journal of Political Philosophy* 20 (2012): 481–498.
16. Of course, anyone who reasonably believes that Russ is stealing Sue's car might be *excused* for interfering, but this is different from saying that such interference is *justified*.
17. Contrary to most criminal lawyers, Douglas Husak is open to the idea that those who have endured extralegal punishment ought to have their sentences reduced. See his "Already Punished Enough," *Philosophical Topics* 18 (1990): 79–99.
18. On this topic, see Alon Harel, "Why Only the State May Inflict Criminal Sanctions: The Case against Privately Inflicted Sanctions," *Legal Theory* 14 (2008): 113–133.
19. Here it is worth recalling Douglas Husak's definition of punishment that I cited at the very beginning of this book. In particular, even though his definition is extremely brief, Husak emphasized that "the very *purpose* of a response must be to deprive and to stigmatize before it qualifies as a punishment."
20. Robert Nozick imagines sadists who roam the state of nature looking for criminals to punish in *Anarchy, State, and Utopia* (New York: Basic Books, 1974), 138.

21. W. D. Ross, *The Right and the Good* (Oxford: Oxford University Press, 1930), 59, criticizes retributivism for generating insolvable questions about how much hard treatment an adult deserves in light of her life's worth of wrongdoing, but the example of Speculative Sadist indicates that the rights forfeiture theory (which Ross preferred) might face analogous problems.

Chapter 7

1. I understand *mala in se* crimes to correspond to actions (like murder) that are wrong in and of themselves, and *mala prohibita* crimes to be actions (like driving on a public road without displaying a valid vehicle registration sticker on one's front windshield) that are wrong only because they have been legally prohibited. As Lindsay Farmer has pointed out to me, even if this construal of the distinction has recently become the orthodox view, *mala in se* originally referred to an idea of crimes as sins, or crimes against nature, in the sense of breaking God's law. According to this earlier understanding, the wrongness of *mala in se* crimes was often thought to be self-evident. For the purposes of this discussion, I do not presume that the wrongness of *mala in se* crimes is necessarily self-evident.
2. I do not mean to suggest that *mala prohibita* crimes pose a problem for only forfeiture theorists. Notice, for instance, that my interest in this question was sparked by Douglas Husak's treatment of the subject in *Overcriminalization* (Oxford: Oxford University Press, 2008), which in turn engages with Stuart Green's article "Why It's a Crime to Tear the Tag off a Mattress: Overcriminalization and the Moral Content of Regulatory Offenses," *Emory Law Journal* 46 (1997): 1533, and R. A. Duff's essay "Crime, Prohibition, and Punishment," *Journal of Applied Philosophy* 19 (2002): 97–108, and all three of these theorists struggle with *mala prohibita* crimes even though none is a rights forfeiture theorist.
3. I am grateful to Antony Duff for this paradigmatic example of a *mala prohibita* crime.
4. For the purposes of this chapter, I shall refer to females who are at least eighteen years old as women and those who are younger than eighteen as girls, whether or not they are mature enough to give their morally valid consent.
5. As Sandra Marshall has suggested to me, if one adopts a normative conception of consent (as the law appears to do), then an immature person's agreeing to something may not count as consent, since there would be no such thing as *immature* consent.
6. Another controversial aspect of statutory rape legislation is the strict liability with which it is often imposed. Thus, even if a man takes every reasonable precaution to ensure that he is not sleeping with a girl under the age of eighteen, he may become liable to punishment if (through no fault of his own) he has

sex with a seventeen-year-old girl. As I indicated in chapter 4, I regard strict liability criminal statutes to be unjust.

7. See my article "Toward a Liberal Theory of Political Obligation," *Ethics* 111 (2001): 735–759.
8. Putting this point in terms of what we owe our compatriots is a little misleading, because I think one would be equally bound to obey the traffic laws in the countries one visits as a tourist, for example.
9. See chapter 4 of my book (coauthored with John Simmons) *Is There a Duty to Obey the Law?* (New York: Cambridge University Press, 2005).
10. Husak (*Overcriminalization*, 112) raises these types of questions about Duff's views on *mala prohibita*. I am grateful to Andrew Cornford for pointing out that, because my view is similar to Duff's, I must also address these issues.
11. A third option would be to split the difference, so to speak, and sentence all statutory rapists to, say, five years in prison. This option appears to be a nonstarter, though, since it would overpunish some, underpunish others, and punish no one proportionately.
12. I am grateful to Antony Duff and Patrick Tomlin for pointing out the potential benefits of this alternative.
13. Daniel McDermott, "The Permissibility of Punishment," *Law and Philosophy* 20 (2001): 431.

Chapter 8

1. Recent abolitionists include David Boonin, *The Problem of Punishment* (New York: Cambridge University Press, 2008), and Michael J. Zimmerman, *The Immorality of Punishment* (Buffalo, NY: Broadview Press, 2011).
2. Similar concerns could be raised about other widely used practices, including solitary confinement.
3. James W. Nickel, *Making Sense of Human Rights*, 2nd ed. (Malden, MA: Wiley-Blackwell, 2007), 44.
4. Douglas Husak, *Overcriminalization* (Oxford: Oxford University Press, 2008), 16. Against this, Vincent Chiao, "Mass Incarceration and the Theory of Punishment," *Criminal Law and Philosophy* 2015, DOI 10.1007/s11572-015-9378-x, has recently argued that, while significant, the war on drugs cannot explain the increased incarceration rates, since the majority of incarcerated people have been imprisoned for committing violent crimes. Even if the majority of those incarcerated have committed *mala in se* crimes, though, the sheer numbers are such that masses of prisoners are being punished merely for possessing drugs.
5. As William Bulow has reminded me, we should also worry about the collateral harms to the family members of those incarcerated. I have never been sure that these collateral harms are necessarily rights violations, and since I want to

be maximally concessive, I would not object that a punishment is necessarily unjust because of those harms. But these collateral harms are certainly relevant in assessing whether the war on drugs is in fact helping the communities it is putatively designed to help. Given the horrible effects of mass incarceration on poor minorities, the prohibition of drugs cannot be justified as necessary (or even the best way) to help imperiled communities.

6. Thus, just as I suggested in chapter 3 that an innocent person who was wrongly convicted is morally at liberty to escape from prison, I believe that someone who is being overpunished may permissibly escape from prison after she has served her proportionate prison sentence.
7. As Tommie Shelby notes in "Justice, Deviance and the Dark Ghetto," *Philosophy & Public Affairs* 35 (2007): 142, "despite making up only 13 percent of the male population of the United States, black men constitute almost *half* of the male prison population, and on any given day, nearly a third of all black men in their twenties are in prison, on probation, or on parole." According to Human Rights Watch, https://www.hrw.org/reports/2000/usa/Rcedrg00-04.htm, "nationwide, the rate of drug admissions to state prison for black men is thirteen times greater than the rate for white men. In ten states black men are sent to prison on drug charges at rates that are 26 to 57 times greater than those of white men in the same state."
8. Shelby, "Justice, Deviance, and the Dark Ghetto," 151.
9. Michelle Alexander, *The New Jim Crow* (New York: New Press, 2010), 51–52.

REFERENCES

Alexander, Larry. "Are Procedural Rights Derivative Substantive Rights?" *Law and Philosophy* 17 (1998): 19–42.

Alexander, Larry, and Kimberly Kessler Ferzan, with Stephen Morse. *Crime and Culpability: A Theory of Criminal Law*. New York: Cambridge University Press, 2009.

Alexander, Michelle. *The New Jim Crow*. New York: New Press, 2010.

Altman, Andrew, and Christopher Heath Wellman. "A Defense of International Criminal Law." *Ethics* 115 (2004): 35–67.

Altman, Andrew, and Christopher Heath Wellman. "From Humanitarian Intervention to Assassination: Human Rights and Political Violence." *Ethics* 118 (2008): 228–257.

Altman, Andrew, and Christopher Heath Wellman. *A Liberal Theory of International Justice*. New York: Oxford University Press, 2009.

Barnett, Randy E. "Restitution: A New Paradigm of Criminal Justice." *Ethics* 87 (1977): 279–301.

Boonin, David. *The Problem of Punishment*. New York: Cambridge University Press, 2008.

Buchanan, Allen. *The Heart of Human Rights*. New York: Oxford University Press, 2013.

Chiao, Vincent. "Mass Incarceration and the Theory of Punishment." *Criminal Law and Philosophy* 2015, DOI 10.1007/s11572-015-9378-x.

Christiano, Thomas. *The Constitution of Equality*. Oxford: Oxford University Press, 2008.

Davis, Nancy. "Rights, Permission, and Compensation." *Philosophy & Public Affairs* 14 (1985): 374–384.

Dolinko, David. "Some Thoughts about Retributivism." *Ethics* 101 (1991): 537–599.

Driver, Julia. "The Suberogatory." *Australasian Journal of Philosophy* 70 (1992): 286–295.

Driver, Julia. *Consequentialism*. New York: Routledge, 2012.

Duff, R. A. *Answering for Crime*. Oxford: Hart, 2007.

Duff, R. A. "Crime, Prohibition, and Punishment." *Journal of Applied Philosophy* 19 (2002): 97–108.

Duff, R. A. "Legal Punishment." In *Stanford Encyclopedia of Philosophy* (Summer 2013 edition), ed. Edward N. Zalta. http://plato.stanford.edu/archives/sum2013/entries/legal-punishment/.

Duff, R. A. "Torts, Crimes and Vindication: Whose Wrong Is It?" In Matthew Dyson (ed.), *Unravelling Tort and Crime*. Cambridge: Cambridge University Press, 2014, 146–173.

Duff, R. A. "Towards a Modest Legal Moralism." *Criminal Law and Philosophy* 8 (2014): 217–235.

Duff, R. A. *Trials and Punishments*. Cambridge: Cambridge University Press, 1986.

Feinberg, Joel. "The Expressive Function of Punishment." Reprinted in Joel Feinberg, *Doing and Deserving*. Princeton: Princeton University Press, 1970, 95–118.

Feinberg, Joel. *Harm to Others*. New York: Oxford University Press, 1984.

Feinberg, Joel. "The Nature and Value of Rights." Reprinted in *Rights, Justice, and the Bounds of Liberty*. Princeton: Princeton University Press, 1980, 143–155.

Feinberg, Joel. *Offense to Others*. New York: Oxford University Press, 1985.

Feinberg, Joel. "Voluntary Euthanasia and the Inalienable Right to Life." *Philosophy & Public Affairs* 7 (1978): 93–123.

Ferzan, Kimberly Kessler. "Rethinking the Ends of Harm." *Law and Philosophy* 32 (2013): 177–198.

Gettier, Edmund. "Is Justified True Belief Knowledge?" *Analysis* 23 (1963): 21–23.

Gladwell, Malcolm. *Blink*. New York: Back Bay Books, 2007.

Goldman, Alan. "The Paradox of Punishment." *Philosophy & Public Affairs* 9 (1979): 42–58.

Graham, Peter A. "In Defense of Objectivism about Moral Obligation." *Ethics* 121 (2010): 88–115.

Green, Stuart. "Why It's a Crime to Tear the Tag off a Mattress: Overcriminalization and the Moral Content of Regulatory Offenses." *Emory Law Journal* 46 (1997): 1533.

Harel, Alon. "Why Only the State May Inflict Criminal Sanctions: The Case against Privately Inflicted Sanctions." *Legal Theory* 14 (2008): 113–133.

Hart, H. L. A. "Prolegomenon to the Principles of Punishment." Reprinted in *Punishment and Responsibility*. Oxford: Clarendon Press, 1968, 1–27.

Hill, Thomas E., Jr. "Self-regarding Suicide." In *Autonomy and Self-respect*. Cambridge: Cambridge University Press, 1991, 85–103.

Hill, Thomas E., Jr. "Servility and Self-Respect." *Monist* 57 (1973): 87–104.

Husak, Douglas. "Already Punished Enough." *Philosophical Topics* 18 (1990): 79–99.
Husak, Douglas. "The De Minimis 'Defence' to Criminal Liability." In R. A. Duff and Stuart Green (eds.), *Philosophical Foundations of Criminal Law*. Oxford: Oxford University Press, 2011, 328–351.
Husak, Douglas. "Does the State Have a Monopoly to Punish Crime?" In Chad Flanders and Zachary Hoskins (eds.), *The New Philosophy of Criminal Law*. London: Rowman and Littlefield, 2016, 97–112.
Husak, Douglas. *Overcriminalization*. Oxford: Oxford University Press, 2008.
Jackson, Frank. "Decision-theoretic Consequentialism and the Nearest and Dearest Objection." *Ethics* 101 (1991): 461–482.
Kamm, Frances. *Ethics for Enemies*. Oxford: Oxford University Press, 2011.
Kamm, Frances. *Intricate Ethics: Rights, Responsibilities, and Permissible Harm*. Oxford: Oxford University Press, 2007.
Kershnar, Stephen. "The Structure of Rights Forfeiture in the Context of Culpable Wrongdoing." *Philosophia* 29 (2002): 57–88.
Lippke, Richard L. "Criminal Offenders and Right Forfeiture." *Journal of Social Philosophy* 32 (2001): 78–89.
Luban, David. "Fairness to Rightness: Jurisdiction, Legality, and the Legitimacy of International Criminal Law." In Samantha Besson and John Tasioulas (eds.), *The Philosophy of International Law*. Oxford: Oxford University Press, 2010, 569–588.
May, Larry. *Crimes against Humanity: A Normative Account*. Cambridge: Cambridge University Press, 2005.
McDermott, Daniel. "The Permissibility of Punishment." *Law and Philosophy* 20 (2001): 403–432.
McMahan, Jeff. *Killing in War*. Oxford: Oxford University Press, 2009.
Miller, Franklin G. "Restitution and Punishment: A Reply to Barnett." *Ethics* 88 (1978): 358–360.
Moore, Michael S. *Placing Blame*. Oxford: Oxford University Press, 1997.
Morris, Christopher. "Punishment and Loss of Moral Standing." *Canadian Journal of Philosophy* 21 (1991): 53–79.
Murphy, Jeffrie G. "Blackmail: A Preliminary Inquiry." *Monist* 63 (1980): 156–171.
Murtagh, Kevin J. "Is Corporally Punishing Criminals Degrading?" *Journal of Political Philosophy* 20 (2012): 481–498.
Nickel, James W. *Making Sense of Human Rights*, 2nd ed. Malden, MA: Wiley-Blackwell, 2007.
Nozick, Robert. *Anarchy, State and Utopia*. New York: Basic Books, 1974.
Oberdiek, John. "Lost in Moral Space: On the Infringement/Violating Distinction and Its Place in the Theory of Rights." *Law and Philosophy* 23 (2004): 325–346.
Pilon, Roger. "Criminal Remedies: Restitution, Punishment, or Both?" *Ethics* 88 (1978): 348–357.

Quinn, Warren. "The Right to Threaten and the Right to Punish." *Philosophy & Public Affairs* 14 (1985): 327–373.

Rawls, John. *The Law of Peoples*. Cambridge, MA: Harvard University Press, 1999.

Rawls, John. "Two Concepts of Rules." In Samuel Freeman (ed.), *John Rawls: Collected Papers*. Cambridge, MA: Harvard University Press, 2001, 20–46.

Robertson, Geoffrey. *Crimes against Humanity*. London: Allen Lane, 1999.

Robinson, Mary. Foreword to *The Princeton Principles on Universal Jurisdiction* (2001), http://lapa.princeton.edu/hosteddocs/unive_jur.pdf.

Rome Statute of the International Criminal Court. legal.un.org/icc/statute/romefra.htm.

Ross, W. D. *The Right and the Good*. Oxford: Oxford University Press, 1930.

Rothbard, Murray. *The Ethics of Liberty*. Atlantic Highlands, NJ: Humanities Press, 1982.

Shelby, Tommie. "Justice, Deviance, and the Dark Ghetto." *Philosophy & Public Affairs* 35 (2007): 126–160.

Shue, Henry. *Basic Rights*, 2nd ed. Princeton: Princeton University Press, 1996.

Simmons, John. "Locke and the Right to Punish." *Philosophy & Public Affairs* 20 (1991): 311–349.

Tadros, Victor. "Consent to Harm." *Current Legal Problems* 64 (2011): 23–49.

Tadros, Victor. *The Ends of Harm*. Oxford: Oxford University Press, 2011.

Thomson, Judith Jarvis. "A Defense of Abortion." *Philosophy & Public Affairs* 1 (1971): 47–66.

Thomson, Judith Jarvis. "Self-Defense and Rights." Reprinted in *Rights, Restitution and Risk*. Cambridge, MA: Harvard University Press, 1986), 33–48.

Tomlin, Patrick. "Innocence Lost: A Problem for Punishment as Duty." Forthcoming in *Law and Philosophy*.

Waldron, Jeremy. "A Right to Do Wrong." *Ethics* 92 (1981): 21–39.

Walen, Alec. "Retributive Justice." In *The Stanford Encyclopedia of Philosophy* (Summer 2015 edition), ed. Edward N. Zalta. <http://plato.stanford.edu/archives/sum2015/entries/justice-retributive/>.

Wellman, Carl. *A Theory of Rights*. Totowa, NJ: Rowman and Allanheld, 1985.

Wellman, Christopher Heath. "Group Autonomy and State Sovereignty." In *Liberal Rights and Responsibilities*. New York: Oxford University Press, 2014, 145–169.

Wellman, Christopher Heath. "Liberalism, Samaritanism, and Political Legitimacy." *Philosophy and Public Affairs* 25 (1996): 211–237.

Wellman, Christopher Heath. "Procedural Rights." *Legal Theory* 20 (2014): 286–306.

Wellman, Christopher Heath. "Rights and State Punishment." *Journal of Philosophy* 106 (2009): 419–439.

Wellman, Christopher Heath. "Rights Forfeiture and Mala Prohibita." In R. A. Duff et al. (eds.), *The Constitution of Criminal Law*. Oxford University Press, 2013, 77–96.

Wellman, Christopher Heath. "The Rights Forfeiture Theory of Punishment." *Ethics* 122 (2012): 371–393.

Wellman, Christopher Heath. "Toward a Liberal Theory of Political Obligation." *Ethics* 111 (2001): 735–759.

Wellman, Christopher Heath, and John Simmons. *Is There a Duty to Obey the Law?* New York: Cambridge University Press, 2005.

Zimmerman, Michael J. *The Concept of Moral Obligation*. Cambridge: Cambridge University Press, 1996.

Zimmerman, Michael J. *The Immorality of Punishment*. Buffalo, NY: Broadview Press, 2011.

INDEX